DENTAL CLAIMSUPPO

Complete Guide to Starting a Dental Practice

Hanging a Shingle

- What to do before and after you open the doors to your practice
- How to set up your business for success starting on Day 1
- How to select a location, get a loan, set up operations, and more

Josh Smith

HIGH BRIDGE BOOKS
HOUSTON

Complete Guide to Starting a Dental Practice: Hanging a Shingle
by Josh Smith

Printed in the United States of America
ISBN: 978-1-954943-49-0

High Bridge Books titles may be purchased in bulk for educational, business, fundraising, or sales promotional use. For information, please contact High Bridge Books via www.HighBridgeBooks.com/contact.

Published in Houston, Texas by High Bridge Books

Contents

Introduction: **v**

Part 1. Is This Really Happening? **1**

1. You're Your Own Boss 3
2. Location 17
3. Creating a Business 23
4. Mortgage and Note 33
5. Vendors and Expenses 49
6. IT Support 95
7. Hiring and HR 101
8. Training 111
9. Competitive Analysis 123
10. Marketing and Advertising 133

Part 2. And so it begins... What happens after the practice purchase? **145**

11. Credentialing 147
12. Fee Schedules 157

13. Practice Management Software 165
14. Your Appointment Book 169
15. Operations and Dental Billing 173
16. Are You Ready? 185

Introduction

Before we get into why this book is called *Hanging a Shingle,* let me be clear about what this book is not. It's not a textbook to bore you. It's not dry, monotonous language. I am bringing humor and personality to mundane dental terms like "fee schedules" and "credentialing" while still giving actionable, research-backed expert advice. Never say never, my friend. Hang with me through my jokes, take the bad ones with the good, because if we can't have fun while doing our life's work, what are we even doing? Okay, back to starting a dental practice.

I've always thought the term "hanging a shingle" was such a cliché. Why not just say, "Hey, I'm starting my own dental practice"?

Sure, it's catchy, but catchy things tend to bother me. But yes, I ended up naming this book *Hanging a Shingle.*

Before you call me a hypocrite, please let me explain.

I hear it all the time in different dental settings. "Sarah is looking to hang a shingle in a couple of months. Isn't that crazy?" Or, "Man, did you hear that? Jamal said his note got approved. He's building a seven-operatory office, his first time hanging a shingle!"

Spare me. I get it, though. Starting out is a *big* deal, no matter how you look at it. It's life-changing. You are your own boss. You are a business owner. You control your destiny (sorry, that was cheesy, but maybe). Anyway, like any new business-owning dentist, I started to realize how important this milestone really is.

I am not a dentist. I never will be. I don't think I could stomach what you do on a daily basis. The blood, the smell, the overall pressure. I just wouldn't be good at it. My strengths are on the business side of running a dental practice. And as a former office administrator and dental billing service cofounder with over 16 years of experience in the field, I do know the ins and outs of a dental office. My partners and I often joke, "We can do everything, except a crown or filling!" No lie, it's the truth.

When my partners and I created Dental ClaimSupport in 2012, we aimed to streamline the dental billing process in offices across the United States. We did just that, but we picked up some other skills as well.

We have built offices from the ground up. We've expanded offices. We've hired administrators, dentists, hygienists, and assistants. We've chosen vendors and ordered supplies and equipment. We've selected dental software, claims clearinghouses, and imaging software. We've handled the billing, negotiated the fee schedules, and tackled the credentialing. We have done the accounting and handled the books. And if you thought of something I'm missing, trust me, we've done it. Brush the dirt off my shoulders, right? I'm kidding!

Seriously though, through it all, we've seen what it takes for a dentist to succeed as a practice and a business, and I'm sharing that with you.

Let's talk about you and other dentists now.

Little did you know that when you went off to college and learned a lot about medicine and anatomy, played way too much beer-pong, crammed for tests at the last minute, attended as many sports events as possible, and slept off your hangover in a.m. lectures, it wouldn't prepare you for what it's really like to be a practicing, business-owning dentist. The fact is that dentists don't get a playbook for life after dental school.

Whether you are building your own practice, renting your own space, joining a practice as an associate, or acquiring an office where you've been practicing, there are multiple levels of responsibility and unknowns that flat out aren't covered—at all—in dental school. Why? Beats me.

But it's the reason for this book.

I have seen multiple dentists struggle to find their place in the dental world following school. Running any business is very difficult. But did you know that only 2% of dentists have a business degree, yet most are business owners? That number should make you stop reading and think for a sec.

Glad you're back. So what's your strategy for success after dental school? Posting a sign above the door isn't enough.

"Hanging a shingle" is an old saying, dating back to the early 1800s. When opening an office, especially a professional practice such as a doctor's or lawyer's office, it was common to say something like, "Juju Smith's renting that office and hanging out her shingle next month." Well, the name Juju Smith probably wasn't too common, but that's where this American colloquialism comes from. (Juju is my daughter's nickname, by the way—shoutout to you, Juju, for all your support!)

Anyway, a "shingle" was literally hung out as a signboard. There's your history lesson for the day.

Okay, let's get back to why I'm not a hypocrite. I'm not a hypocrite because building a business is no different than building a house. Therefore, "hanging a shingle" is actually quite appropriate.

What does a house need? It needs a solid foundation. It needs to work for people. It needs to run well to serve a purpose.

What does a dental office need? It needs a solid foundation. It needs to work for you and your patients. It serves a purpose!

So, my question to you: Are you ready to go on this journey? I hope you are. I urge you to use the information in this book to set yourself up for entrepreneurial success.

Being a dentist is about fixing teeth and creating confident smiles. It is by far one of the most important occupations we have as humans. People will always have teeth, and mouths will inevitably be in pain. However, being a business owner is not about fixing teeth and smiles. Being a business owner is about income and profitability. It's about creating jobs, running lean, and having a positive impact. It's about growth and stability. I know you can be both an effective dentist and a successful business owner. This book will help bridge that gap and marry your dental expertise with dental business know-how. So take a minute to put away your scrubs and settle in. It's time to take off your dentist's hat and put on your business owner's hat.

Let's do this.

Part 1

Is This Really Happening?

It is happening ... It's a wonderful feeling being a business owner, and you are going to begin that journey.

Part one of this book focuses attention on what happens before the practice purchase and how it's actual done. You'll also understand the necessary basics to stay mindful of before you walk in those doors on day one as the new boss.

1

You're Your Own Boss

Yep, this is really happening. You're starting a dental practice, and it's probably the reason you are reading this book. I hope it is anyway.

Before I get this chapter underway, I want to make something abundantly clear.

YOU CAN DO THIS!

There has been a shift in recent years of fewer and fewer dentists being sole owners in their practices. Why? Well, dentists nowadays have more debt coming out of school, and the risk may be too high for them. Or, we have these large groups or DSOs (dental service organizations) saying, "Hey, new dentist, owning a business is *just too hard* … why not come work for us?"

I'll show you. Here is a graph from the American Dental Association showing the decline of dentists in private practice from 1999 to 2021. Keep in mind, these are solo practitioners.

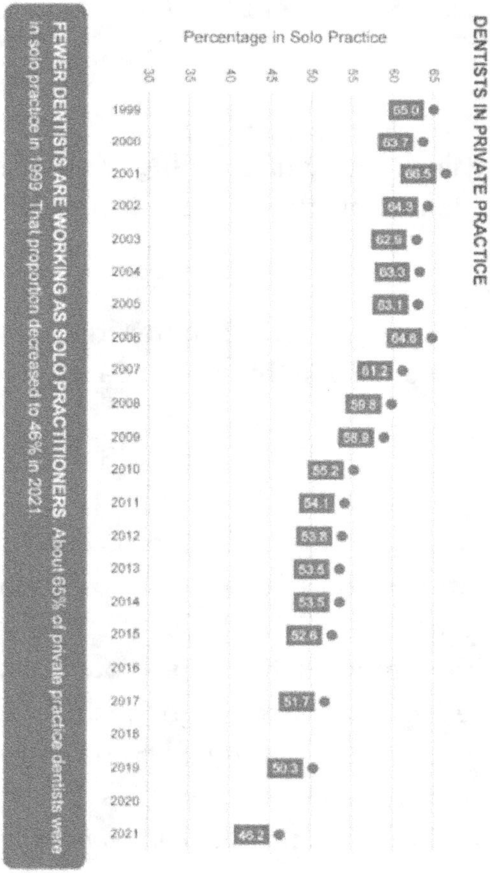

Image from www.ada.org

As you can see, the percentage of dentists in solo practice has dropped from 65% in 1999 to 46% in 2021. That is an overall 30% drop in 22 years. Is it substantial? Yes. Is it surprising? No. It's not. It's not because our world is changing. Insurance is far more difficult to deal with now than in years past with ever-changing policies, fine-print, and regulations. Human resources and finding the right people have become more difficult with a shift to the digital remote world. But don't let this scare you.

These are challenges you can overcome, and I'll show you in this book. Shoot, close to 50% of dentists still own their own practice, and you can add to this number. Yes, it can be appealing to start out as an associate, make some cash, and learn the ropes; personally, I am not against this. But that does not mean you can't eventually own your own gig, especially if you know what you're up against.

Allow this book to tell you what you need to know. Let's get back to it, shall we?

This chapter will focus on real-life ways dentists find their ideal offices, how pricing is generally determined, and how to ensure the dental office fits your goals for the future.

You would never hear a dentist, right out of school or seasoned, say finding the right practice isn't important when starting their entrepreneurial journey. It should be. Chances are you aren't some dental office "flipper" filming your latest episode on the DIY network. No, you are probably looking for your permanent location to set up shop, fix smiles, fill your pockets, and retire to Aruba.

So if this is you, ask yourself a few questions.

Is the office located where you want it to be? Is it the size you want? Does the price point make sense? Are you thinking about the future? Could this be your forever spot? We will dive into these questions further, but these are all questions you want to consider and check off your list.

Finding a Dental Practice

It may seem daunting, but finding a practice is honestly not that difficult. As stated already, the majority of dentists coming out of school choose to become associate dentists to get their feet wet. This way, they can learn the ropes and be a sort of well-paid apprentice.

It's not a bad gig. They are doing the work and gaining experience but earn a paycheck without the headaches of running a business, dealing with the accompanying stress of personnel and HR problems, or having to actually write the paychecks themselves.

But let's say you are one of those few coming out of school and want to set up your own shop. Or let's say you are one of those who have already been in the associate game, honed in on your skills, and have decided to go out on your own. How do you go about locating an existing practice for sale? There really are two fundamental ways to go about this.

1. The old school way: Write letters to all dentists in town. Yes, this is still done today. Look online, talk to mentors and colleagues, or network to get a feel for who may be a potential seller in the present or future. Create a form letter that can be easily personalized. Letters may reach someone on just the right day. This could be a dentist that is just ready to retire, wants to relocate, or is burned out. Also, your letter is

something they can keep and reference later if they are willing to sell. And what does that cost, maybe $100 to send to 50 different dentists? It's cheap, easy, personable, and leaves a lasting impression.

2. Networking: Meet others at dental meetings, lunches, and dinners. Most dentists are members of local dental societies. Dentists are a close-knit group, so use that to your advantage. Also, network with sales reps and see if there's gossip about anyone who is selling or who is close to retirement age. Make it known that you are looking to purchase. *Trust me,* once it's known that you are looking for an office, opportunity will come your way, and you will receive help from others that have been in your shoes. Again, dentists are close-knit and help each other out.

All this is fine and dandy, but there's something you should know. Dentists are stubborn when it comes to selling. Sorry to break it to you!

I heard it from a dentist I know: "Dentists are all crazy when it comes to selling. They all want to sell, but they don't want to sell." If that sounds ass-backwards to you, that's good because it is.

Most dentists decide to retire when it becomes a physical need. Their eyesight may have diminished, they may have back and neck problems, or they just want free time. Other than that, they just keep working even though others, and possibly themselves, would say it's time. Don't let this be a discouragement. Just know it's not uncommon to get many nos before you find your yes.

When you've succeeded in waking the right dentist from their "I'm never selling" coma, you need to nail down the timeline for when the sale will go through. Discuss an agreed-upon deadline or date range when the selling dentist will relinquish some or all ownership, depending on the deal. **Always realize that it will take longer than what was agreed to**. Did I just bold that? Yes, I did! For whatever reason, this seems to be the case. Be conservative and add one to two months to this timeframe for your own sanity.

Lastly, the dental community, believe it or not, does a damn good job of having tight lips once a deal has been discussed. Most of the time, deals made between sellers and buyers stay very silent until the ink has dried on the contract. I stated earlier that the dental community helps out one another, and that's still the case. But once you've found the right fit and after deals are made, don't spoil your own deal by talking about it too much. Loose lips sink ships in war and in business dealings.

How is the sales price determined?

You will *always* need to get a professional evaluation of the practice. This is usually paid for by the seller. We'll discuss more of this in chapter four, but here are some basics to consider. Evaluations will typically require tax returns for the past two to three years for the practice and the annual gross revenue for the previous three years (showing how much money per year has been collected).

Once these numbers are determined, practices sell on average for around .7 or 70% of that annual three-year gross revenue. In some locations with higher income for dentists and a higher standard of living, that factor will be more like .99 or 99%. Let's explain this a little further in the example below.

Example: If the average yearly income of your practice were $1 million for the previous three years, your practice would likely sell for around $700k on average and $999k on the high end.

Why isn't this higher? Great question!

What are some factors affecting sales price?

Patient Count

Well, the reality of the situation is that the office will most likely lose a few patients (what some bankers call "patient run-off"), and revenue will decline a little once a new doctor takes over. Dentists are no different than primary physicians when it comes to patients. Patients find dentists they like and stick with them.

Also, the new doctor may not participate with the same insurance companies as the previous doctor. This means that patients having these particular insurance policies have to choose whether they stay and pay more out of pocket or find a dentist that does participate.

Productivity

Depending on the experience and skillset, sometimes the new dentist can't begin producing at the same level as the previous doctor because more experienced doctors typically offer more advanced procedures and often have higher case acceptance because they have developed trust with their patients.

Also, if acquiring a practice the new doctor has never worked in, other variables such as new staff, unfamiliar territory, and new patients present production challenges until comfortability sets in as time passes.

Assets That Convey

Most dentists are selling the business, but not the property/real estate. They don't own the property, only the business. This is something to keep in mind as the seller. It's the business being evaluated and sold, not the building or land you are on.

So when purchasing a practice, not only will you have to actually buy the business, you will still need to pay rent to who owns the land or building.

Asset Health (Especially Accounts Receivable)

We just spoke of some obvious factors affecting sales price, but what are some other curveballs you may see in the sale of a practice? Some dentists try to make "acquired A/R" a selling point when selling their practice. What I mean by acquired A/R is how much money patients and insurance companies still owe to the previous doctor after the new doctor has taken over. I mean, wow, it sounds great, right? Are you telling me I didn't even do the work on these patients, but I can get the money for it? Essentially, yes, but acquired A/R is negotiated in the sales price and presents its own challenges. Old balances are difficult to collect on, from patients and insurance companies, and can disgruntle these patients. You never know what the situation really was or how this old A/R was being handled before you set foot in your new office on day one.

My recommendation: Don't fall for this acquired A/R trap. If the previous doctor couldn't collect it, how is the new one going to?

You do need to negotiate who receives the money that is still rolling in from patient payment plans, old invoices to patients, and outstanding insurance claims.

One option: You can set up an end date for payouts to the selling dentist for money coming into the practice. This cutoff is typically the date the new dentist started. Therefore, any payments dated before the start date of the new dentist can go to the former dentist. This is done off the honor code, though, as the previous doctor doesn't have access to your software system and bank account. I know what you're thinking, but don't be a swindler! I've seen this happen and hurt the previous doctor.

Some dentists make it a true "turnkey" situation. They stock up on supplies for the new dentist and ensure all equipment has been serviced and is up-to-date. It's almost equivalent to buying a house after having an inspection, with the seller fixing anything needing repair, paying the closing costs, and stocking your beer fridge. How generous!

What does your dental team look like?

The standard dental team for a start-up dentist includes two hygienists, one or two administrative employees, an assistant, and of course, the doctor. A beautiful little family of five or six. This means that the dental office typically has two operatories for the two hygienists and two ops for the dentist, with maybe one overflow.

Think hard about how you want to structure your practice. The amount of space you need will depend on if you built a practice from the ground up or purchased an existing one. You will not have 3,000 patients in your books on day one if you build a practice from scratch (unless, of course, you are bringing them from a different location). Added space means added expense. Therefore, there would be no need for 10 operatories. Catch my drift?

However, leaving room to create more ops or just not equipping certain ops can easily be a solution to decrease expenses if you choose to build.

If purchasing an existing location, there are many ways to add space if you are looking to expand. You won't need the space immediately, but if you are the go-getter doctor looking to add an associate in the future to increase revenue, make sure your location is sufficient to house more operatories with renovating. Or guarantee you have room to build out, increasing square footage. This would need to be discussed in the purchase and agreed that renovations and increasing square footage are approved.

So where is this office going to be, anyway? Let's talk about that next.

2

Location

The first three words in any real estate textbook are location, location, location! To put it lightly, location is important. The beauty of dentistry is that it's needed everywhere, except England maybe. Come on! I promise I'm just kidding!

In all seriousness, give some thought to where your practice is located. A lot of times, this applies more to building a practice. Because if you are purchasing a practice from someone else, you should already be familiar with the revenue and have a good idea of what to expect based on the patient base and existing location of the office.

Here are some personal pro tips to think about when it comes to location:

1. **Which major employers are located in the area?** Most dentists accept insurance. Big employers typically provide great insurance benefits, and most employees don't want to miss too much work for any type of appointment, especially dental work. Employees will stay close to the office, meaning they will look to find a dentist in close proximity to their workplace. You can simply ask around or get in touch with HR departments at large companies to figure out their dental insurance carrier. It's amazing what picking up the phone can accomplish.

   If you participate with their insurance, they are more inclined to come to you. You participating with their insurance means they get in-network discounts. People love discounts. It's that simple.

2. **Is the area already saturated with other dentists?** This can be good or bad. Areas already saturated don't need another drop in the bucket, so to speak. If the area isn't growing

and already has too many dentists, your pool to pull from gets shallow. Keep your finger on the pulse of this. You can easily look up dentists per capita in your area and do basic math to determine if demand is still there for more dentists.

On the other hand, sometimes dentists' offices can be sort of like mattress shops. You know what I mean? Mattress shops seem to be next to other mattress shops. Seriously, like four or five in a line. If you haven't noticed this, I urge you to look for this next time you're on the road. CVS is almost always on a corner with Walgreens next door, too. This is known as Hotelling's law of spatial competition in economics.[1] It states that businesses that sell similar products or services are located close together in order to obtain maximum market share.

If a few dentists are clumped together, the idea is that they at least share the market equally, as opposed to being the outlier that doesn't draw as much traffic in an area that isn't as highly commercial, with flourishing restaurants and businesses. Think about the dentists who set up in a shopping mall around a bunch of different businesses. Seems odd, but in actuality, it's very smart. I'm including specialty dentists in this example too. Oral surgeons, endodontists, periodontists, etc. can benefit from being located around general dentists because general dentists will refer to them for special treatment. If you want to nerd out more on Hotelling's model, check out this link below and view the video on Ted.com.

ed.ted.com/lessons/why-do-competitors-open-their-stores-next-to-one-another-jac-de-haan

3. **Is there a good mix of commercial and residential buildings in the location?** I hit on this a tad in the last point, but if you can have a location close to housing, apartments, *and* businesses, you should have no issue building your patient base. How

convenient your practice is to where people live and work is a huge factor in whether they make an appointment.

4. **Is the location up-and-coming or stagnant?** This is also something discussed briefly, but don't start your entrepreneurial career in an underpopulated location. It seems like common sense, but I've seen it *a lot*. Yes, there are small towns everywhere in the United States, and everyone needs dental care. This is true. Just ensure you are the only, or one of the few, dentists or specialty dentists in these situations. There are only so many mouths to feed. Pun intended.

[1] ed.ted.com/lessons/why-do-competitors-open-their-stores-next-to-one-another-jac-de-haan

3

Creating a Business

Once you have found the perfect fit, grab your accountant and grab your lawyers. You will need them to handle the legal matters of acquiring the practice. Everyone tends to know somebody that knows somebody that knows somebody. You know?

If you have never used or had your own accountant or lawyer, ask around, and find accountants and lawyers that have experience in this area. We have already discussed the network that dentists live in, so lean on the network for referrals or recommendations for your accounting and legal team. Remember, you may be looking to acquire a dental practice from someone else and not start a brand new one, so surely even that dentist has a recommendation.

Accountant: I don't mean you need an accountant at your office banging away at a calculator. However, accountants will be instrumental in estimating what you can take home monthly as profit. Meaning what's left over after you pay off the note each month, overhead (employee payroll), lab costs, supply costs, all other vendors, and all other expenses.

This estimate is easier to achieve if you are purchasing an already-existing establishment rather than opening the doors of your own start-up.

Lawyers: Most practice owners will have one lawyer to create your business entity (probably an S-corp) and possibly one more to aid with the contract negotiation of buying/selling the business. Yes, you are a smart dentist, but please leave negotiations and legal formalities to the experts and let them handle it.

Create Your S-corp

Creating a business really isn't that difficult. It's actually very cheap, and you can technically "start" a business, with paperwork, for only a few hundred dollars.

Your lawyers will show you the ropes and handle all the paperwork. By this point, you know many of the important basics. For instance, you know where your practice is, if you are building or purchasing a pre-existing business, and what your debt will be. Remember, "mortgage" means debt. It's a loan. But that's why it's essential to have a good accountant and lawyer on your side to talk you through what to expect when you open your doors. Mortgage and note will be covered in the next chapter.

So back to the type of business entity. I recommend an S-corp for a few reasons. But first of all, what is an S-corp?

By definition, an S-corp or (Subchapter S corporation) is:

> A special form of corporation that allows the protection of limited liability but direct flow-through of profits and losses[1]

Like anything in life, an S-corp has advantages and disadvantages. The main reason I recommend an S-corp for dental offices is that the advantages far outweigh the disadvantages.

Very simplified, S-corps protect the shareholders (you) and their assets from creditors should your business be in debt. Basically, they can't come after your personal bank accounts, house, car, pontoon boat, or baseball card collection. That was a test. Are you still with me?

S-corps do not pay federal taxes at the corporate level, and they shield the business from taxes by passing taxes through to shareholders to file on their personal income tax returns. Lastly, S-corps are easy to create, transfer ownership, or disband.

Here's a nice little list for you of advantages and disadvantages:

Advantages

- **Protected assets**: creditors can't come after your personal bank accounts, home, or other personal assets
- **Pass-through taxation**: no federal taxes at the corporate level
- **Tax-favorable characterization of income**: shareholders (you) are paid by salary and distributions. This can

reduce self-employment taxes and have the business incur expenses and wages paid as deductions for the corporation. Taxes are simply filed on your returns, and the business takes the expenses hit, lowering your taxable income.

- **Straightforward transfer of ownership**: buying and selling made easy, and that is great news for dentists
- **Cash method of accounting**: S-corps are typically $5,000,000 or less in income annually. This means you can use a cash method of accounting. Cash method basically means a real-time snapshot of revenue and expenses rather than anticipated revenue and expenses. *Much* easier for the business owner—you!
- **Greater credibility**: When your business is incorporated, some people view it as more credible. Basically, you have made a formal commitment to your business. This can be

attractive to certain vendors or partners because it demonstrates your commitment.

Alright, those were the advantages, so let's now hit the disadvantages. I list them all out and provide a peek into my brain on what I believe the disadvantage means in actuality to you. I think you'll see why S-corps are a great fit for dentists. Let's see.

Disadvantages

- **Formation and ongoing expenses:** The business has to be incorporated by filing articles of incorporation. Articles of incorporation are "a set of formal documents filed with a government body to legally document the creation of a corporation. Articles of incorporation generally contain pertinent information, such as the firm's name, street address, agent for service of process, and the amount and type of stock to be issued."[2]
    - **Reality:** This takes a little time (not much) and costs you a little

cash (not much, though). It's also handled by your lawyers. Perfect!

- **Tax qualification obligations:** paperwork and info on stockholders need to be accurate, or the S-corp can be shut down
  - **Reality:** This is very rare. Again, you are the shareholder, so there's no reason this info should be inaccurate
- **Calendar year:** tax year runs as a calendar year and *not* a fiscal year
  - **Reality:** No biggy
- **Stock ownership restrictions:** can only have one class of stock and also only 75 or fewer shareholders
  - **Reality:** You are a dentist ... I highly doubt you will have 75 shareholders. You may give ownership to an associate(s) or various business partners, but not 75 of them.
- **Closer IRS scrutiny:** because of the tax savings and how an S-corp

works, the IRS will pay a little extra attention to an S-corp to make sure things are on the up and up

  - **Reality:** Handle your affairs accurately, pay your taxes fairly and timely, and this isn't an issue. You have an accountant already, right?!

- **Less flexibility in allocating income and loss:** 99% of the time, you are the only owner; therefore, allocating money to only one person is easy
  - **Reality:** Having very few owners means this disadvantage doesn't really apply to dentists
- **Taxable fringe benefits:** fringe benefits, or a perk offered by an employer that is above and beyond someone's annual salary or other wages, is taxable to shareholders owning 2% or more of the business. Basically, you pay yourself a salary or distributions when you own your own S-corp, so these fringe benefits are paid to you anyway and are taxed on your personal returns.

- **Reality:** Again, this isn't really a disadvantage because *you* are paying *yourself* more with distributions or bonuses. You are taxed one way or the other.[3]

Alright, there you have it. S-corps may not be the best fit for everyone, but they are a great fit for dentists. The advantages are self-explanatory, and the disadvantages don't affect dentists significantly whatsoever.

Your choice, of course, but you read it here. If you plan on owning a massive DSO (dental service organization), then you need to think differently. But is that what this book is really about? Nope!

[1] www.entrepreneur.com/encyclopedia/subchapter-s-corporation

[2] www.investopedia.com/terms/a/articlesofincorporation.asp

[3] www.wolterskluwer.com/en/expert-insights/s-corporation-advantages-and-disadvantages

4

Mortgage and Note

I mentioned in the previous chapter that mortgage simply means "debt." Yep, you are borrowing a substantial amount of money that needs to be paid back. Your note literally works the same way as a mortgage on a house.

This is extremely important, so stay with me in this chapter. No one really loves to discuss debt service, collateral, interest rates, EBITA, LTV, and other scintillating financial acronyms, because it's boring. But I will do my best to simplify this process and make it as interesting as possible. Research wasn't exactly fun for this chapter, so I'll go ahead and thank Savannah, Georgia's South State Bank executive, Travis Thomas, for his help!

I sat down with Travis and asked him exactly how a business loan works.

First, Travis says that all situations are different. The most common scenario you see is a younger dentist graduating from school and going to work for an established dentist for several years (or longer).

The conversation of transferring ownership eventually takes place, and they come to an agreement for the new dentist to buy out the previous dentist's book of business and FF&E (furniture, fixtures, equipment), or basically the office and everything in it.

Banks are typically more comfortable with this scenario because there is an established cash flow stream that can be analyzed and measured to repay the proposed debt, and the risk of patient run-off (patients leaving) is more minimal in the bank's eyes as the patients are familiar with the new dentist already. You will see a common "risk-averse" theme throughout this chapter on mortgage and note when banks are referenced. The less risk they take on, the more inclined they are to lend more money at better rates. Keep that in mind.

Banks also get additional comfort when the retiring dentist agrees to work for a period of time after the sale. Banks call this a "practice loan." Another favored scenario includes a "practice buy-in" through which a dentist is buying only a percentage of the practice.

Although the first is a common scenario, you still see dentists go out and purchase other practices after working at a different one. So the only difference is they are purchasing the business from a different doctor and not one they worked with. The same information on "how a mortgage and note work" still applies for the purpose of this chapter.

Let's look at what the typical structure might be.

Collateral

When buying a full practice, banks would almost always take what's called a "blanket lien on business assets." This is a UCC-1 (Uniform Commercial Code) court filing giving the bank basically any asset the practice has as collateral in the event of default on payment. The more collateral, the better, obviously, but the bank would likely be primarily interested in the value of the physical equipment: dental chairs, pano machine, computers, etc.

This is trickier if only buying a portion of a practice as the other doctor(s) may or may not be willing to pledge the assets (this sometimes depends on how much they want this new dentist). Requiring an assignment of the dentist's life insurance is also common and helps strengthen the credit. For example, if this dentist were to die, those proceeds would go first to pay off any bank loan. Yeah, it's morbid but makes complete sense.

In some cases, if the bank still wasn't totally comfortable with the credit profile. In the bank's eyes, maybe they think they are paying too much, or amortization (the period of time to pay off the loan) is too long, or there's a lot of risk of losing patients. There could be a request for further collateral: a second mortgage on your primary residence, a spouse's personal guarantee, etc.

Loan Amount and Down Payment or LTV (Loan-to-Value)

If a bank is very comfortable with a deal, financing 100% of the acquisition price is not uncommon. Pretty cool, right? Obviously, the more money you put down, the better terms from the bank you can get, such as a favorable interest rate. If the bank has a little heartburn for whatever reason, they may ask that the borrower come up with a 20% down payment.

Debt Service Coverage Ratio

Another factor in the loan amount is what a bank calls its "debt service coverage ratio." Banks will look at existing practice financials and confirm that there is a history of ability to service your loan payment with what is referred to as EBIDA (earnings before interest, depreciation, and amortization). To get you a little in the weeds here, the ratio is basically:

(Net Income + Depreciation + Interest Paid + Amortization) / All Loan Payments

1.25 x EBIDA would be a good industry standard here. Do you see why it's good to have a competent accountant? I thought you might.

Terms/Structure

This can really vary from deal to deal, but Travis says a dentist should probably be prepared to pay back the debt on a seven-year schedule. It can often be increased to 10 years if needed. Please note that these are the norms, and not all situations are the same.

Any dentist can pay this back sooner, but it depends on cash flow. This is easier for dentists that acquire an already established practice with a patient base. You would simply figure out what your net profit is at the end of every month and find out what percentage of revenue is your net profit. If you aren't comfortable with doing this yourself, either through spreadsheets or programs like Quickbooks, then have your accountant explain your profit and loss (P&L) statement to you.

If you are comfortable with paying more toward your principal, then do that to decrease the overall term of the loan. However, depending on your interest rate, you always need to consult with your accountant about whether this is the right move. Paying extra to your principal every month or quarter, or whatever you choose, will obviously eat into your working cash that you may otherwise use to hire employees, buy more product, buy more equipment, use personally, etc.

Everything mentioned thus far in this chapter would be typical for acquisition of any already existing practice. Next, we will hit on a scenario of starting a brand-new office either by renting a space or an office that was built from scratch.

What about a dentist starting their own practice and not purchasing from someone?

Another scenario is a dentist who just wants to rent an office space and start completely on their own.

This scenario is a little bit tougher. The dentist would really want to have experience as an associate somewhere to show their ability to produce, meaning perform dental work and create revenue. If not, the LTV (loan-to-value) could potentially not be 100%, and the dentist could be looking at second mortgages on a primary home and/or pledging any other hard collateral, possibly including a bank CD. As a side note, specific dental equipment financing from a bank is probably five to seven years, industry standard, with a 0% to 20% down payment.

Remember, banks love guarantees. So if you can't show them these guarantees with reports of your ability to perform dental work and create revenue or any historical data, then you will have to provide more collateral. A brand-new start-up with a first-time practicing dentist would fall into this scenario. It's the nature of the beast.

It's also recommended to obtain a small line of credit when getting started. It would likely be cross-pledged, meaning the same collateral we discussed earlier would be used as the practice loan. This can be used to fund short-term working capital. One important thing that dentists sometimes don't realize is it is *not* appropriate to finance fixed asset purchases with a line of credit (i.e., equipment, furniture, whatever you wouldn't pay off within a month or so). The most traditional use of this line of credit is for account payables to vendors and also payroll expenses.

It's tempting to use a line of credit as permanent cash, but they are usually 12-month commitments. So if at the end of 12 months you have what banks call a "stale balance" on the line, it's very likely the bank will make you take out a new loan to amortize that balance over one to three years. A stale balance is basically the portion of the debt left on your line of credit that can't be paid off by combining cash on hand and conversion of your receivables from patients and insurances.

A line of credit should only be used when waiting on receivables from patients to convert to cash, and then the line should be paid back.

One Other Note

That pun was intended! Anyway, when buying a practice from a retiring dentist, there can very often be a seller-held second loan position. For example, with a $750,000 loan, the bank will lend $500,000 to the dentist at agreed-upon terms and then pay the retiring dentist that $250,000 over their own agreed-upon timeline (say maybe 10 years at 5%).

Banks really like this scenario because it lowers their leverage and keeps the retiring doctor with some skin in the game. It's appealing to the seller, too, because it gives them an annuity of sorts at a decent return (much more than they can get in a CD at the bank). It can also have tax advantages, such as possible tax-free income.

Alright, you now have that extremely riveting rundown of how it all works. Let's get into a few more details of how to set yourself up for success with this loan process and what to be prepared for.

What does a dentist need to have prepared for this loan process?

A lot was covered already related to preparation, but you need some other things to complete the process. Here we go!

- Get your personal tax returns ready.
- Get a personal financial statement ready.
- Analyze existing practice financial statements before agreeing to a sales price. This ensures you are comfortable and can live off of what will be left over after you start paying the debt service.
- Anticipate any upcoming potential capital expenditures needs: replace older equipment, chairs, office remodel, etc.

- Take all of that and have at least three to five-year projections of where the practice will be financially.
- Take into account some patients leaving and get comfortable with a worst-case revenue scenario. It's always good to be conservative when planning financials. If you are prepared for patients leaving and possibly losing that already consistent revenue, yet your worst-case scenario is still profitable, then you will be okay.

I would engage a CPA or specialist early to help with all of this. *Do you see why it's good to have a competent accountant?* Oh my, I said it again...

What are the typical interest rates for these loans?

Interest rates change too often to stay true in writing, so don't quote me. However, interest on a strong dental credit practice loan is probably in the 3.25% range right now (as of January 2022). But it could certainly be higher.

Fixed rates have typically been within half a point of WSJ Prime. What is the WSJ Prime?

> The initials stand for The Wall Street Journal, which surveys large banks and publishes the consensus prime rate. The Journal surveys the 30 largest banks, and when three-quarters of them (23) change, the Journal changes its rate, effective on the day the Journal publishes the new rate. It's the most widely quoted measure of the prime rate, which is the rate at which banks will lend money to their most-favored customers. The prime rate will move up or down in lock step with changes by the Federal Reserve Board.[1]

If you are trying to start "de novo," then expect to pay more interest and have a higher interest rate. De novo means "from the new," so you don't have to look up the definition. Don't you wish more people did that for you? You can thank me with a five-star review!

How long does the entire loan process take to make the funds available for purchase?

Approval can probably be done relatively quickly, depending on the bank. As long as there are no real estate and equipment appraisals to be completed, 30 days should be reasonable. Don't let anyone drag their feet here, and certainly don't drag your own. Keep the process moving with consistent communication. I said in an earlier chapter to conservatively add one to two months to this process, and I stand by that. But it can be done faster if all parties have their Daffy Ducks in a row.

Pro Tips I'll Leave You With

1. Smaller banks move quicker than bigger banks with the loan process. Seek options and pick what fits into your desired timeframe for acquisition.
2. The more money you put down, typically the better interest rate you get.
3. The less risk the bank has, the better interest rate you'll get.

4. Purchasing an existing practice with historical data typically carries less risk for the bank.

5. Renting space or building your own practice typically carries more risk for the bank. Remember, no historical revenue data for the bank makes it riskier for them.

Lastly, for this chapter's purpose, I asked my buddy Travis at South State Bank the following question:

"If you could give a dentist some inside scoop on what to look for, what would it be? What are ways the dentist could get burned in this process or charged too much? Basically, knowing what you know, if your best friend was a dentist and was getting a loan, what advice would you give?"

Aside from everything already discussed, Travis says, "Ultimately, try to develop a trusting relationship with a banker, and you should be in pretty good shape. A good one can really guide you through this process. Medical loans are deals banks want overall, so terms should be favorable. You could also get two-term sheets from different banks for comparison. That is a little more work, but when getting started is a good idea."

There you have it. These are all things most people, not just dentists, aren't necessarily taught. It's all life-learned. Use this mortgage and note information to confidently approach the lending process. In essence, know what you're getting into and what to expect. All sales/purchases are different! But with a good basic knowledge of how this works, you'll be ahead of the curve, trust me.

[1] Bankrate: www.bankrate.com/rates/interest-rates/wall-street-prime-rate/

5

Vendors and Expenses

Get out your wallets, people! You are running a business now, and guess what? Everyday services you never thought about before are now expenses to be aware of when it comes to business.

This isn't to scare you; it's to keep from getting blindsided. All dentists use vendors and have tons of expenses but are still very profitable. It's just important to know that commercial expenses, as opposed to residential expenses, seem to bring a higher price tag.

This chapter outlines the various vendors you may use when running your dental practice. Although you may use more or fewer of these vendors, *pay attention* to your books and what's going out—meaning what you are paying in expenses each month.

Be frugal, but don't be cheap. There are ways to save in areas by doing a little bit of research, negotiation, and staying smart with your choices. Some quick examples are simple things like merchant fees for credit card payments (which we will also discuss in detail in this chapter).

You will no doubt need a credit card merchant unless you only accept Bitcoin. But seriously, there is a myriad of credit card merchants out there, so do yourself a favor and do some research and negotiate. You need a credit card merchant in order for patients to pay by credit card. Don't pay 3% per transaction when you can pay 2.5%. It all adds up.

This is what I mean by "be frugal, but don't be cheap." You will find that this premise can apply to each of these vendor categories I will discuss. Too many times in my career, I've found money being thrown out the window. This can be because a dentist allows an office manager to handle all the vendors and doesn't have a pulse on it, or whoever is in charge of vendors and expenses has let some things fall through the cracks. Let me give you a few examples so it hits home. I've seen:

- Dentists paying for two imaging (x-ray) software services and not knowing it
- Dentists paying for two clearinghouses instead of one (claim submission software)
- Dentists paying for monthly magazine subscriptions (never used)
- Dentists paying for extra computer stations where a hygienist or assistant would work (never used)
- Dentists paying for monthly extra voice over IP (VoIP) phones (never used)
- Dentists paying for dental software reporting/data companies (yet don't do anything with numbers given)
- Dentists paying for two practice management softwares (PMS). You only need one … Trust me!
- Dentists employing too many front desk administrators

Things like clearinghouse services (how dental claims are sent to insurance companies) can cost $100–$300 per month (or more depending on the size of the practice). Imaging software and extra phones can run you at least $50 per month each. These examples are to remind you that once you are running your business and making decisions, little things like an extra phone nobody uses can fall through the cracks and *cost you money*. It's easy to lose sight of these little things when they aren't on your radar.

Alright, let's settle in and talk about the many vendors you may encounter as a dentist. *I literally took these vendors from a dentist buddy's Quickbooks system.* He is a solo doctor with two hygienists, two assistants, one office manager, and a ton of dad jokes. And for that reason, let's call him Dr. DadJokes, or Dr. DJ for short.

Note: *The vendors I will discuss are standard in dental offices, but when I get into average costs, such as supplies and lab costs, I am using the averages from Dr. DJ's actual expense report. All numbers averaged from quarter four of 2021.*

Supplies and Supply Company

Average Monthly Supply Costs: $2,500–$3,500 (Based off Dr. DJ's office)

Always get quotes from multiple supply companies. More quotes equal better options.

If you find you can buy supplies directly, do it. Think of this like the Carvana model. I'm sure I don't need to explain the whole used car salesman joke, but with Carvana, you don't deal with a middleman. Thank the heavens! This means you aren't paying for a salesman's commission.

It's no different with dental supplies. If you go through a sales rep, you will undoubtedly be charged more as the sales rep collects a cut of the purchase price. To combat this, you can use something like Saftco (saftcodental.com) or Darby (darbydental.com) and buy direct.

We all know the big guys in the industry. If you want to go the Patterson or Schein route, make sure you meet with the local sales reps. Give them 10 main dental products you know you will use, and let them duke it out for your business. Create some sort of spreadsheet for each company and compare the pricing. Who has the best deal? They all say they provide value and service, but guess what? It's all the same stuff!

Same companies, same manufacturers. Companies like Patterson and Schein offer the same stuff.

Once you've come to a decision, then spend your money on what really matters. For example, buy quality composite and cement. What goes in a patient's mouth is what matters the most. Again, be frugal, but don't be cheap.

Lab Company

Average Monthly Lab Costs: $2,800–$4,000 (Based off Dr. DJ's office)

Every dental office has to use a lab. Choosing a lab doesn't have to be hard. Your choice could very well depend on the quantity of products or quality. Most dentists choose their lab by a visit from a lab company salesman, word of mouth, or online research.

Some labs specialize in certain products: implants, zirconia crowns, removables, or orthodontics. It takes trial and error to find what works for you, as there are three main variables. We'll get into how to choose the right lab for you later in this chapter.

I'll feature the lab company, Pan-Am, in this book as I have a personal relationship with their director of sales, Jimmy McIntire. Jimmy is horrible at fantasy football, but he's been with Pan-Am in sales and customer satisfaction for over 10 years, is an outstanding person to work with, and takes great care of his doctors.

I was able to sit down with Jimmy and get the skinny on what you need to know when choosing your lab. Our aim was to be unbiased and give you this information straight. The three main variables you need to consider are:

- Service
- Quality
- Price

These are bulleted in no particular order. Why? Because what to look for in a lab is different for everyone. Yes, there are dentists out there that could give a rat's ass about quality and simply want the lowest price. Some dentists put their eggs in the service basket, knowing that they will always have the lab to lean on when it relates to a difficult case or particular patient, talking cases through, or continued education. And some other dentists just want "the crown to fit," and if the quality is right, who needs all the communication?

Think about who you are and what matters to you. Here's a fact: Many labs are great, but none lead in every category. Larger labs provide better pricing because of bulk. They are producing so many units that pricing undoubtedly goes down because of quantity. However, local labs, though typically higher-priced, can provide a personal touch and possible one-day service. With these basic examples in mind, let's talk about the three main categories when choosing a lab.

Service

Service is arguably the most important factor when choosing a lab (to me, at least).

Service is a big thing. Before now, it used to be one lab tech owned their own shop and took care of 50+ dentists regionally. Labs have always been an extension of the doctor's arm, and that's still the case today

Included in service are:

- Training
- Turnaround time
- Support
- Trust
- Education

- **Training for dentists and teams**: Yep, some labs do this. They talk with major manufacturing companies—3M, for example—and open them up to their customer base. This is a win-win for the lab and the manufacturer. First of all, 3M now has up-sale potential by talking about their impression material. But second, 3M also trains dentists and assistants on taking impressions properly to solidify what the lab is looking for. This is free training that leads to fewer remakes and more time saved for both the dentist and the lab.

- **Turnaround time**: This is a big one. Neither doctors nor their patients want to wait long to receive their crown or denture, right? Lab cases don't need to be rushed because quality would go down, but there is certainly a sweet spot for timeliness. What is your desired turnaround time?

- **Support**: (Labs should tell you what you are doing right or wrong, especially for new dentists.) If you're having bad luck with cases, how does the lab respond? Are they simply saying, "Oh well, send it again"? Or are they addressing the problem and figuring out why the crown might be coming "high" every time. Could it be prep, and is the lab articulating that to you?
- **Trust**: Is the lab going to be there when poo hits the fan? Do they have all the products you need? When you call, is there someone there that knows who you are and what you are talking about? Relationships are built on trust.
- **Education (10 over 10 rule)**: This is a phrase Jimmy, from Pan-Am, likes in the lab business. It means 90% of remakes are coming from 10% of a

> lab's customers. Some labs will just fire the dentist and find another customer. Other labs may make the investment in your office and educate your dental team in order to avoid these remakes. Good labs will do the latter.

I really hate saying this, but here we go … dentists are the main culprit when lab cases are not working or fitting. This is real data, and labs have the photographs to prove it. It's a delicate conversation because dentists never make mistakes, right? On the flip side, there are some bad techs, but let's be real: lab companies don't like remaking cases! It's costly. Labs monitor these techs and figure out who may have the highest percentage of remakes, and guess what? That tech probably won't be cashing many more paychecks.

Remember, the lab only has what you give them. It's all digital. They pour up your model or impression, scan it, and are going to be within 3/10th of a micron of accuracy. (Trust me, I didn't know what that meant either!) Here's Jimmy's example for clarity. Count a couple of grains of salt, and it's smaller than that. What I'm saying is labs take what is given by the dentists and use high-tech machines. Things are digitized, so other than the pouring up part, labs are digitizing that model and milling based on that CAD (computer-assisted design) file. It's about as accurate as it gets.

Quality

Let's talk about remakes. The industry average of remakes is 6% to 8%. Yes, this means that 6% to 8% of anything dentists send off to the lab needs to be redone. Either it didn't look right (color, shade, quality, etc.), or it just didn't fit the patient. Most good labs can cut that down to 3% to 4%. Pan-Am, for example, operates at 3.5%. With the adoption of digital dentistry, offices are getting scanners directly from companies like Henry Schein and leaning on them for quality. This helps the lab.

Price

Pricing is, of course, different with each lab. It also depends on where you are in the United States, as the standard of living plays a part in this. From what you've learned already, your best pricing will likely come from larger labs.

It's all a matter of what you are looking for, though. My best advice is to shop around.

Most labs give free cases in order to earn your business. Jimmy recommends doing a trial run of five cases. These five cases are typically fixed appliances, such as zirconia or emax (what the majority is composed of today). With the "try five" rule, the dentist sees the quality, understands the pricing, and experiences the turnaround time. If it's a fit, go with that lab.

Note: If you used a lab once and the contacts were off, give them a shot to fix it. One try is not a very fair assessment for any lab.

I stated earlier that local labs are usually a bit higher in price, but why? Take a look at these reasons listed below.

Local labs are known for:

- Quick turnaround and fewer logistics, same day service
- Crowns in two to three days
- Personal touch
- Difficult shade cases

Is there anything wrong with paying more to use a local lab? Nope. Is there anything wrong with paying less to use a larger lab? Nope. Just make your own decisions here after trying them out.

From his personal experience of the many dentists he's helped, Jimmy is an advocate of having a go-to lab for the majority of your cases but also having another lab (local or large) on the side for specific cases. Maybe you need a quick turnaround or you're having issues with getting an anterior tooth shaded correctly. This is when you can call on your local lab, pay a little extra, but get the correct expedited product for your patient.

What is the future of dental labs, and how does technology play in?

Fact: Lab technicians are aging out and starting to retire. The average certified dental technician (CDT) in America is around 55–60 years old. Skilled removable technicians are even harder to come by, and there are only a few places left teaching this trade.

Labs (the good ones) have started training from within and buying mom-and-pop labs for the intellectual property. However, the trend is overwhelmingly moving towards digital and CAD/CAM capabilities.

A major thing to look for in any lab is how they are keeping up with the times. Are they integrating new technologies into their laboratory? Like we said earlier:

Digital = Less Human Error = Less Remakes

Dental artificial intelligence has not replaced human discernment yet. So far, labs have not bridged the gap, and CDT's quality control and troubleshooting skills are still essential to business.

Lastly, are the lab personnel knowledgeable, willing, and able to train you and your team on your own technology for restorative work? As mentioned earlier, training is a huge part of the "service" portion of choosing a lab. It's a necessity now more than ever. Why?

Because a lot of these scanner companies will come in, drop off a $50k scanner, train you for an hour on the aligner technology, then bail without touching the restorative side of things. Do you really want that type of service? I think not.

We've covered more about labs than you probably even wanted to hear. I know this is riveting stuff, but let's wrap it up.

For the book's purpose, I asked Jimmy to put together a quick process for dentists to follow when making a decision on which lab company to use.

Here's the process for you:

1. You need to do a risk-free trial with a rep in the area. The lab doesn't have to *physically* be there but should have someone that can come in and help.
2. Check quality.
3. Check pricing.
4. Check support and what the lab provides outside of the tangibles. Great communication and customer service. Do they provide education when it may be needed?
5. Make a decision.

Remember that labs are in the business of getting it right the first time, no different than dentists who want to avoid redoing work on a patient. There's always been pressure on labs to "just get it to fit" and deliver, and that's *not* good in the long run for dentists, labs, and most importantly, patients. Work with your lab and have an open dialog should you ever hit snags. Good labs can usually isolate and fix any issues quickly through communication and skilled quality control.

Jimmy put it quite bluntly to me. "In the lab business, you're only as good as your last case."

This brought me to say, "Well, maybe dentists are only as good as their impressions." Just saying! It's not a one-way street.

Equipment

Equipment is expensive in dentistry, and it seems like everyday items, such as cabinetry, have an inflated price. Some people actually go to a place like Ikea and get a free designer to plan the cabinetry configuration and pay a fraction. Some people utilize garage cabinet companies to build their dental cabinets. I'm not kidding. The cabinets are no different, though. A cabinet is a cabinet, and don't try to change my mind.

Also, places like Ikea have warranties on their products. This means if something is faulty, they will replace it. Or if cabinets just give out in 10 years, just buy them again. Enough about the cabinets. Moving on.

Let's talk about different equipment. Going back to chapter four, equipment can be acquired in the purchase of a dental office and it is categorized as FF&E (furniture, fixtures, equipment). This includes anything from couches to x-ray machines and dental chairs. For the purpose of this chapter, let's discuss dental chairs.

On the dental chair front, I recently, in 2021, heard of a quote of $67k to install a dental chair for one room that's already plumbed and wired with electrical. This is one operatory, people! Don't get swindled. There are many options.

Beyond purchasing the chairs with the practice, you can also buy refurbished equipment with a warranty, save a ton of money, and have top quality. Some companies, such as Atlanta Dental or Patterson, will ship a complete chair with everything on it, all equipped, for around $10k–$15k. The chair will last 15–20 years too. Installation is nothing. It's all self-contained. Just get someone strong to put it in the room, plug in the power, click in the water, and boom—it's money-making time!

If you don't want to go the refurbished route, you can, of course, buy new. Accountants will be able to depreciate the equipment for you over time. Thank you, handy accountant.

Lastly, you can lease equipment and include this expense in your loan, discussed in chapter four, as well. You decide, but the rule of thumb is: Don't go with your first quote. Do your research, and then do what's right for you.

Credit Card Merchants

There is a litany of credit card merchants. They all literally do the same thing, but some may cost you more monthly than others. Listed below are certain things to consider when choosing a credit card merchant.

- What are the fees and other costs of using credit card merchant services?

  - **Interchange fees**: This refers to the fee charged for every transaction. It typically ranges from 2% to 3%
  - **Monthly fees**: These are literally fees tacked on to invoice you. Dumb, I know. These can range anywhere from $10–$20 a month. They can be negotiated too
  - **Application and setup fees**
  - **Monthly minimum fees**: With most merchant companies, there is a set floor or minimum amount you need to meet. For example, if fees only add up to $125 for the month and your minimum is $150, your merchant will charge you the additional $25.
  - **Early termination fee**: "What, you want to leave us? Gonna have to charge you for that!"
- How long will it take to get set up? Merchants can be set up on the same day or within 48 hours.

- What are the accepted payment types? (i.e., American Express, Visa, Mastercard, etc.)
- Does the merchant accept new payment technologies? Maybe they offer direct deposit setups for patients.
- How helpful is customer support?

Like anything, get quotes. Give the merchants a made-up number of transactions along with a made-up dollar value of the sum of these transactions. The merchant should be able to provide a hypothetical invoice on what that cost would be. Make your decision after these comparisons.

Medical Supplies

Things like nitrous oxide are not ordered from your normal dental supply company. This is something to keep in mind if you want to keep those patients gassed up, feeling easy, and thinking everything is funny! Seriously though, some patients truly need nitrous, and it makes the "dreaded dentist's office" a doable experience. Like everything else, though, it floats a bill.

Other medical supplies you may need are:

- Meds for emergencies (Epi-pens, reversal agents, etc.)
- Oxygen tanks
- First aid kits
- Monitoring equipment (for blood pressure, pulse-ox, etc.)
- Defibrillator
- Wheelchair

A fun quote I heard from a dentist once was, "Man, you need a lot of medical stuff I didn't think about when I opened my practice, but keep all that crap hidden so you don't scare people!"

I thought that was pretty funny, but maybe I'm weird. It's true, though. If some anxious patients see all your medical supplies for "just in case" scenarios, it may make them more nervous. Best to keep these behind closed doors and out of plain view.

Plumbers and Electricians

Yep, if you have running water and electricity, you're bound to have an issue at some point. Ask around and choose a credible company, and also one you can have a relationship with. As stated earlier, things typically get to be more expensive when it's a "business," but your plumbing and electricity have to be serviced. You literally can't run your practice without either.

Software (practice management software, clearinghouse, imaging software)

Software, such as your practice management software (PMS), clearinghouse (electronic claim submission), and imaging software (digital x-rays) carry expenses.

PMS is paid for on a monthly basis and can run anywhere from $100–$500 depending on the software. There can also be other fees associated with your PMS, such as monthly support for questions on how to use it properly, update it, or fix bugs. We will dive into PMS in detail in chapter 14, so stay tuned.

Clearinghouse software is paid on a monthly basis too. Clearinghouses are essential to your practice as they are the means of getting dental claims to the insurance company, electronically, in order to get you paid. Take a look at www.dentalclaimsupport.com/blog/best-dental-clearinghouses to find a clearinghouse that fits your practice.

If you don't have one, you will be mailing claims daily. I shouldn't have to get into how expensive, time-consuming, and idiotic that is.

Clearinghouses typically charge a flat monthly rate, then tack on an additional rate per claim submitted. Some have fees higher than others, and some have different features (like insurance verification and eligibility), so doing your own research to find the one that fits best for you is imperative.

Imaging Software

You can't live without it. There are many imaging software on the market, and some work better with certain PMSs. Imaging software is essential for keeping every patient's x-rays in order by date and type of x-ray.

Imaging software is necessary for getting certain claims paid, such as crowns, bridges, implants, dentures, and more. If you don't have x-rays to document and justify a patient's procedure, insurance has the right to deny the claim. Not fun, and not cool for your wallet.

City and County

Taxes, permits, licenses (I'm in Georgia, and these are updated every two years. In other states, it's every two to four years.)

Utilities and Miscellaneous

Below is a basic list of dental office utilities to expect. There isn't much more on this topic besides paying attention to the bills each month. Always look for spikes on any invoice. For example, if your water bill went from $75 to $150 in one month, you have a problem. Oftentimes, this is something an office manager would monitor if they are responsible for accounts payable.

- Water
- Electric
- Internet
- Phones
- Office alarm
- Waste pickup
- Landscaping
- Pest control

Some miscellaneous expenses could be the following:

- Shredding company
- Magazine subscriptions
- Office lunches or parties
- Continuing education

Memberships

As a dentist, it's beneficial to be a part of various dental memberships. For the third time, dentists are a tight-knit group. Memberships provide the ability to network, mingle, and bounce ideas off of each other.

Most memberships are at the local, state, and regional levels and are usually referred to as "dental societies." Listen, to be 100% honest, I'm not huge on the networking thing, but

I've been to many different dental society meetings to speak and present, and they are actually fun. Members are engaging and are there to build relationships and help one another. Good food and booze never hurt either!

Information Technology (IT)

I will go into more detail in chapter six about IT. However, this will be a monthly cost to you as well. Your IT costs will include:

- Website creation and maintenance
- Website domain
- IT company
    - Server setup
    - Server backup
    - Workstation setup (computer, printer, scanner, etc.)
    - Security and monitoring
    - Software setup (practice management software, claims clearinghouse, imaging software, and x-ray setup

- Being the IT "voice" for your office for other vendors or installs. Your IT company should be able to speak for you in matters of technology with other vendors.

Dental Billing Company

It's my book, so I can say this. I'd be remiss if I didn't mention outsourcing dental billing companies, like Dental ClaimSupport (the best outsourced billing company). This is an expense you would need to consider if you use it for your dental practice. For accounting purposes, remember that expenses are write-offs to your business, meaning all expenses limit your taxable income. Among all the other benefits, this means that outsourced billing companies cost much less to you than hiring someone in-house to do the billing. Just saying…

Outsourced dental billing has become much more of the norm in the dental world. It's an advantage to have your dental team focused on your patients while an outsourced billing team handles all the insurance headaches (claim submission, payment posting, researching outstanding claims, appeals, etc.) and ensures you get paid.

Outsourcing isn't for everyone, but it has saved dental offices across the country that truly didn't understand the ins and outs of the dental billing process and were hemorrhaging money. Many dentists decide to outsource, and it's for various reasons. Maybe collections are way down. Maybe they had a key employee leaving, such as an insurance coordinator who handled all the billing. Maybe they had consistent turnover. Maybe the current team just wasn't getting the job done, and the outstanding A/R continued to snowball.

Outsourcing your billing is also something you can delegate off your plate since you're worrying about everything else we've outlined so far in this book. Whatever the reason, making the decision to outsource isn't an easy one, but it's no different than other business decisions. Do your research, ask questions, and weigh the pros and cons.

I suggest heading to Dental ClaimSupport (dentalclaimsupport.com) to read all you need to know about outsourcing, good and bad, so you can educate yourself and make a decision that fits your needs

Insurance

Before I get into the various insurances, I want to give a special shout-out to Tim Blanco, a partner at Chatham Insurance in Savannah, Georgia (https://chathaminsurance.com). Tim and his team specialize in providing essential insurance to dentists, and I personally know a plethora of dentists in our hometown of Savannah that utilize and trust Tim's services. He's my go-to dental business insurance expert, so obviously he was the go-to professional for this information.

Most of us are the same when we hear the word "insurance." It makes us squeamish and uncomfortable. For many, it's because we aren't educated in insurance, and people naturally fear what they don't know. Many would rather stick their heads in a hole like an ostrich and hope everything magically goes away and ends up okay. That's a term called "ostriching."

In the real world, though, and when owning a business, ostriching is not an option. So, with Tim's help, I'm here to say: You are not an ostrich, so don't act like one. Glad we cleared that up.

If you've picked up on a major theme in this book, it's that I want to give you real-life, unbiased information, so you can make your own decisions as a dentist and what's best for you. You will feel better about your apprehension and understanding of insurance by the end of this section.

One of the mistakes that dentists frequently make is the commoditization of insurance. But guess what? It's not a commodity; it's a necessity. It's not a product or job to be bid on, have five quotes thrown at you, and you inevitably take the lowest price. Trust me, you'll get what you pay for.

As Tim put it, "The devil is in the details, and while many insurance products have very similar foundations, there are significant differences in structure."

Please remember that quote. What Tim is saying is sure, there will be a lowest price. There always is. But what coverage are you actually getting? Pay attention to the details because that lowest price you want to take may not be the coverage you actually need.

Everyone has a friend or family member in the insurance business. Many dentists rely on the agent recommended by the local dental association. What you probably don't know is the dental association gets kickbacks from these recommendations. Yep, you read that correctly.

For instance, I am located in Georgia, and the Georgia Dental Association (GDA) has an owned insurance agency within it. Therefore, association recommendations are normally purchased or are a revenue stream for the association. The GDA solely contracts with two insurance providers, but I'm not naming them here. Having this insurance agency within it creates revenue for the GDA, but it's not always the best coverage for the dentist. Why? Because your practice's unique needs are rarely heavily vetted.

You may choose and want to use an agency that has broad market access with specialized knowledge of the dental industry. This will be critical to your long-term success. Ask other dentists for referrals and interview agents. Selecting the right agent to structure your program is imperative to achieve the broadest coverage at the lowest price. You need an agent that specializes in dental practices and has contracts with many companies to meet your evolving needs.

As a start-up, other initial policies that you will need to consider and include are:

- Commercial package
- Workers' compensation and employer's liability
- Commercial umbrella
- Professional liability
- Cyber liability
- Employment practices liability

I'm about to break these down for you and do my best to tone down the insurance jargon. As Tim put it, "Insurance can be as clear as mud!" So I am going to filter it as much as possible for you.

This is precisely why Tim encourages dentists to engage a specialized agent!

I'll wrap up this section with a chart providing price ranges for these coverages. The price ranges are educated guesses and are based on our example of a *five-operatory, 3,000-square-foot dental practice*.

Here goes nothing!

Commercial package: this can be referred to as a business owner's policy. This policy is rated off of property limits and general liability exposure. In a nutshell, your insurance quote is calculated based on the size of your practice, the number of operatories, and/or square footage.

Commercial package is the most common policy a dentist or practice owner would purchase. It's made up of two key coverages: property and general liability, with property containing some support sub coverages.

Let's break down property and general liability coverages:

1. Property: These are all the first-party coverages for your "stuff."
    a. Building: if you own the location or are required by your lease to insure the location itself. This can pertain to the roof, walls, etc.
    b. Business personal property: sometimes referred to as your "contents." This can include your computers, equipment chairs, etc.
    c. Business income/extra expense: loss of income from a covered event (i.e., fire, lightning, smoke, wind, etc.)

2. General liability: This is coverage for being sued by others for damage to their personal property (except for malpractice—we'll cover this later).

Alright, so you now have the basic breakdown of commercial package. We've discussed that this policy includes property and general liability coverage. It can also include equipment breakdown, hired and non-owned automobile liability, and cyber coverages. If you own your location, you can include building coverage in the package.

Let's now discuss how you can arrive at a certain dollar amount of coverage based on our example dental practice.

- Under item "b" under property, earlier I mentioned, "contents" (or business personal property insurance) means all the stuff inside the practice that you own but is not the building itself (which you may not own). This policy should be written to ensure that it includes additions and alterations to the building. Setting a contents limit for coverage is very important. So how do we arrive at a number? A general rule is to use $70,000 per operatory, and then add another $50,000 for general property. What I mean by general property is property such as certain computers, phones, x-ray equipment, tools, desks, chairs, etc., not assigned to an operatory.

- From our general rule ($70,000 per operatory, and add another $50,000 for general property), here's our example: a five operatory practice would need $400,000 in coverage.

  (5 operatories x $70,000) +
  $50,000 (general property) =
  $400,000.

- Flood and earthquake coverage are specifically excluded coverages and not covered in commercial packages. You should work closely with your agent to understand the risk associated with your location(s) and the cost of buying insurance for that risk.

Workers' compensation and employer's liability: This coverage protects you against work-related injuries or illnesses to your employees or yourself. In most states, it is not only property risk management but a legal requirement to have workers' compensation coverage. If your practice is in multiple states, make sure that each state is listed on the policy.

Normally, the owner has the option to be excluded from workers' compensation coverage. This line of coverage is inexpensive, and the rate applied to owner compensation is capped. Therefore, do not be tempted by the small premium savings. Keep yourself included in the coverage. You never know what can happen to you while on the job.

Side note: Workers' compensation premiums are subject to an annual audit. Yes, this is annoying, but it makes sense because workers' compensation premiums are based on payroll, which likely changes yearly. Comply with the audit, so you don't subject yourself to premium penalties or canceled coverages.

Commercial umbrella: A commercial umbrella is extra liability coverage for your business and sits above other policies. A commercial umbrella can be written inside of a commercial package but typically stands alone. It is wise to have excess liability limits that sit over your commercial general liability, commercial or hired and non-owned automobile liability, employers liability (workers compensation), and professional liability. You likely want to consider higher limits, but at a minimum should have a $1,000,000 umbrella.

Don't confuse this with personal insurance. Your personal insurance includes policies such as homeowners, auto, and personal umbrella insurance. Tim has heard dentists say, "I have a personal umbrella policy." Well, that's good, but that personal umbrella policy will not cover any issues related to your business.

Professional liability: When possible and for ease, it is recommended that your professional liability (malpractice) coverage be placed with the same company that has your commercial general liability coverage, mentioned earlier under the "commercial package." It is imperative that you as a professional and the entity(ies) are covered on the policy. The professional liability policy should be structured to include coverage for your staff, including hygienists and techs. It is also important that you obtain a copy of the professional liability policy for any independent contractors, associate dentists, or locum practicing in your office. Their limits should be equal to or higher than the limits that you carry on your professional liability policy.

Pertaining to your professional liability, there is a significant difference between an "occurrence-based" and a "claims-made" insurance policy. Let's define these two policies.

An occurrence-based policy has lifetime coverage for the incidents that occur during a policy period, *regardless of when the claim is reported*.

A claims-made policy only covers incidents that happened and were reported *within the policy's time frame.*[1]

www.businesscredentialingservices.com

Most insurance companies push the claims-made versus the occurrence-based because it limits their liability. For a multitude of reasons, *always pick the occurrence-based option when available*. This type of policy costs a little more, but it's well worth the fractional additional premium.

On that note, the most common coverage limit is $1,000,000 per occurrence and

$3,000,000 aggregate. Aggregate simply means the max the insurance will pay during one policy term. For example, you could have three $1,000,000 claims or six $500,000 claims., if you had a $3mil aggregate.

Cyber liability: This coverage can frequently be added to the commercial package or Businessowner's policy. The forms have yet to be standardized by the insurance industry and vary significantly from company to company. This coverage can include first-party or loss of income and damage to your system and third party which is compensating people for damages caused to them from a breach.

In a digital world, the protection of patients' personal health information (PHI) and personal identifiable information is difficult. The dental office's protection is also imperative. Having this coverage is a must for every dental practice.

Employment Practices Liability – This is coverage for wrongful hiring, termination or not hiring or terminating. This coverage can be tailored to extend to third party claims. Sadly, allegations of inappropriate actions are hard to prevent. Insurance companies have set up systems to help guide you through what to do and also the defense network to respond.

What does all of this cost you? Check out the table showing price ranges so you can get familiar with these expenses. *These are estimated annual payments, based on our example, five-operatory, single-location practice.*

Coverage Type	Price Range (low to high)
Commercial Package	\$1,300 to \$2,200
Workers Compensation	\$750 (based on \$325,000 payroll)
Commercial Umbrella	\$500 to \$1,000
Professional Liability	\$1,000 to \$2,250
Cyber Liability	\$500 to \$1,500
Employment Practices Liability	\$250 to \$1,500

I hope your brain doesn't hurt too badly. Business insurance policies is that topic we have to discuss, but let's be honest: No one really wants to. Take the info you've learned here, and use it to ask the necessary questions when obtaining these various policies.

Aside from the different coverages already discussed that are mainly related to the protection of the dental business, physical dental office, personnel, and patients, keep in mind there are other additional human resource-related coverages to consider for the staff.

- Employee health insurance
- Dental and vision insurance
- Accident policies
- Possible insurance on retirement plans: 401(k)
- Short-term disability
- Business continuity: This is disability coverage underwritten on the dentist, but provides loss revenue to the practice. Short-term disability insurance replaces revenue for the dentist, but business continuity insurance replaces revenue for the practice. It helps maintain the value of the practice, keep the practice running and

help hire and staff temporary positions while the doctor is recovering. It can also help position the practice to sell.

- Long-term disability: Many doctors make sure they have these policies in the event they permanently get hurt and can't work, have issues with their hands, etc. When you are the income generator for your family and running a business, you need to protect yourself! This also protects your employees should they have an extended absence from work for various reasons.

As Yogi Berra said in the old Alfac commercial, "If you get hurt and miss work, it won't hurt to miss work." Man, that's a classic.[2]

Ok, you're done. Take a break … I get it.

Marketing Vendors

The various ways dentists market are below. We'll cover marketing in more detail in chapter 10, but these things also add up. Dentists need to market in order to attract new patients and generate revenue:

- Insurance marketing (getting credentialed and in-network with insurance companies)
- Ad words (Google and social media)
- Radio ads
- Mailers
- TV commercials (This is rare. Not many dentists do commercials.)
- Billboards
- Magazines
- Business Cards

Postage

Limit your postage as much as you can. Many dentists like to send mailers out, either for marketing purposes or to remind patients about their appointments. Don't waste your money here. There are better options that save you time and money.

There has been a shift to digital marketing efforts that work. Companies like DemandForce or VYNE Trellis can help with email campaigns, appointment reminders, and text marketing. In our day and age, your patients won't mind these methods either. Email and text are the norms, but if customers would rather not be reached by email or text, they can just opt out, and your office will need to phone them.

We also mentioned clearinghouses earlier. *Always* send your claims electronically. They will get to the insurance company faster, you will get paid faster, and you won't be wasting money on stamps from mailing claims.

[1] www.businesscredentialingservices.com

[2] Ibid.

6

IT Support

IT support can be one of the last vendors you select for your office. Once you have a server and need backups, a firewall, and virus protection, you'll need someone to help you maintain all these things. Note: you'll still need IT support if you use a web-based practice management software.

Interview a few IT companies and get quotes. Prices and services are all different, but it's all about what you need or want. Don't get hosed by IT companies and be sold on services you don't actually need.

Below I've listed the two most common ways IT companies support dental offices.

1. Managed service
2. Break/fix

Managed Service

A good low-end monthly rate for IT support can run $300–$600 as a package to cover and support a dozen computers. What I'm describing here is your typical five to six operatory office with five to six employees (including the dentist). So adjust accordingly based on the number of employees and work stations you may end up having.

With managed service, most IT companies will charge per user, per device, or sometimes both, depending on the situation. It's full-service and all-inclusive. Sure, you might only need something fixed or have some sort of install or issue three to four months out of the year, but you're safe and secure and have the support you need.

Also, with managed service, servers usually cost more than the other typical work stations. For example, a managed server might be $100 a month and $30 for each workstation. Other devices can include firewall appliances, printers, scanners, switches, or anything connected to the network.

Basic managed services would include monitoring, updates, and usually unlimited remote support. Keep in mind, though, that things like anti-virus, malware, ransomware, or other security offerings could be extra or in the next "tier" of service.

It's safe to say managed service is mostly a "you get what you pay for" type thing. The low end is already about $25/device. If a company tells you they can do it for $10/device, your service is probably going to be lackluster.

Lastly, make sure you shop around if this is the type of service that you want. Big city/higher standard of living locations are going to cost you more. It's the nature of the beast.

Break/Fix

Break/fix is exactly what it sounds like. Break/fix is essentially when you call an IT provider or take your broken equipment to one, and they charge you an hourly rate plus the cost of parts to—you guessed it—*fix* it!

For comparison reasons, in a case like this, most items would have been covered under a managed plan minus the cost of the part if needed. And with break/fix, you would be floating the cost of basically everything. So, think of managed services more like an insurance policy or warranty, and break/fix as paying out of pocket as needed.

Needless to say, both types of IT support for dental offices work. It's just a matter of what you feel you need. Some dentists out there are highly skilled in IT or have an employee skilled/nerdy enough to handle the majority of the IT support needed in the office. In this case, they may opt into a break/fix arrangement as it suits them better.

However, most dentists and their teams need help. What I'll leave you with is don't overpay and be swindled.

I've heard of offices shelling out $2k–$3k monthly for IT support, and this just isn't necessary. We've discussed IT services briefly, but listed below are a few things you will use your IT company for:

- Server setup
- Server backup
- Workstation setup (computer, printer, scanner, etc.)
- Security and monitoring

- Software setup (practice management software, claims clearinghouse, imaging software, and x-ray setup
- Being the IT "voice" for your office for other vendors or installs

You should now have an idea of what you should look for when it comes to IT. I'm sure you can agree that there are ways to set yourself up and be secure, and none should carry a $2k–$3k price tag retainer per month.

7

Hiring and HR

Hey, Doc! You still with me? Good, be-cause to me, this is the most important chapter in this book: hiring and HR.

You will see that the next chapter goes right into training your dental team, but training is pointless if your team doesn't have a good attitude, work ethic, and a patient-minded focus.

I suggest having most of your team on deck or fully in place three to four weeks before you open your practice. This goes for building your own practice or purchasing a current practice.

This builds in enough time just in case your new office manager, administration team, assistants, and hygienists have to give notice at other locations. Your interview process may take at least two weeks to meet different candidates and find the right fit. Carve out 30–45 minutes for interviews. Lunch meetings work well for this if your future candidates are working elsewhere. Your objective is to assess not only the candidate's ability to get the job done but also professionalism, trainability, trust, and work ethic. You want them to be a good fit, not just with yourself but for other employees, your patients, and your overall vision of your business.

You may also inherit a dental team if you purchase an existing location. Remember, this is your practice, so treat the personnel situation seriously but delicately. You are the new kid in town, but in this case, the new kid is calling the shots, right?

It's imperative to get a lay of the land before you start working with your inherited dental team. Open for a day and do not see patients, but use the day to establish an office relationship and begin alignment. Discuss what the day-to-day will look like under you. Meet individually with each person, and get their personal feedback on how things have been going and what their personal roles and responsibilities include. Treat it like a "get to know you/evaluation."

This is your opportunity to let them know what you expect from them, but it's also your opportunity to sympathize with them and address that you know this is a change for them too. Bringing any new employee, even a new doctor, into the mix comes with its own set of challenges. Change is difficult for some, and you are most likely not going to operate the same way their previous dentist did. You may have a different managing style. You may have a different structure to your day. You may implement new processes. The earlier you get this out in the open, the better your relationship with your dental team will be. They need to know that you are not who the previous doctor was.

Ok, let's get into the nitty gritty…

Flashback to high school, everyone. Dental offices are known for being cliquey. Certain employees like to set up silos. Man, I hate that word—silos. Silos are divisions in your office in which people operate independently and close themselves off from other employees. For example, I've seen hygienists team up against assistants or front desk admin separate themselves from the clinical team. This will hurt your practice. It's not that it's just bad for morale and the overall culture of your business, but your patients notice it too. Many times, this can stem from one bad egg that creates the division between teams and employees.

If you notice a bad egg in your office, get rid of it. This is the person with a bad attitude. This is the person talking negatively about other employees or you, for that matter. This same person is a pot stirrer and talks employees into not liking another employee. This person outwardly creates conflict and is argumentative with co-workers and doctors in front of patients. This person also has the uncanny ability to complain to or in front of a patient about their job or another employee. There is nothing more unprofessional than that.

I can't believe I'm writing about this at my age, as we are way beyond high school, but it's true. One individual can seriously harm your practice and squeeze the life out of it. So if you see this type of behavior, squash it.

Full disclosure: I had the exact employee I was just discussing in my own office, and I let it linger too long. I made multiple mistakes in hiring early on in my dental career too. I'm a people person. I like everyone to be happy with their job and role, and I constantly look for the good in people. That's all rainbows and butterflies, but don't approach hiring like this! It will bite you in the ass.

As for the bad egg, address the behavior. Meet with your team, ask questions, and eventually the truth will come out about a certain employee or employees.

Would your team be more energized and efficient without this person? Would your patients be happier, possibly? Do you have an employee cross-trained to take over responsibilities if you let this person go?

These are difficult questions to ask, but you are the business owner. You will be faced with these decisions from time to time. So keep this in mind. Happy employees, positive environments, and increased morale always trump hanging on to a subpar employee you are scared you can't survive without. Cut the bad fruit off the tree, and make the sacrifice!

Avoid the bad egg by hiring the right people. Candidates need to be vetted. Do not hire someone on the spot. You need to have a hiring process and do your best to follow it. At my company, Dental ClaimSupport, we take our potential employees through an eight-step hiring process (sometimes longer):

1. Application to work
2. Pre-screen phone-call
3. Exams and assessments
4. Zoom interview
5. Zoom interview #2
6. In-person interview
7. Reference calls
8. Contract call

Does this sound like too much to you? It may, but it's incredible what you begin to learn about someone the more you meet them, talk with them, ask them questions, and put them in behavioral situations.

Basically, the candidate either gets the job or talks their way out of one.

You can cut out a couple of steps in the process I listed for your own sake of time, such as Zoom interviews or the contract call, but my point is to just be as thorough as you can with hiring. Taking more time to hire the right someone will save you loads of time in the future with less turnover and training.

Here's a quick hiring pro-tip: *When hiring, have a role you are hiring for, then hire someone to fit that role. Don't hire someone, then give them a role.*

What I'm about to say, I could say five more times, just to get the point across…

You will not have a successful practice if you do not have the right personnel in place.

I know I already discussed the pot-stirring employee, and I stand by that being the biggest problem in any workplace. However, your dental team also needs to know what they are doing. Too many times, I see dentists hire individuals with absolutely no experience, work ethic, or trainability. Even if an employee is coming from another dental office, find out why, and test their knowledge of their specific role. And remember, always check those references! It's amazing what you can find out from previous employers, the good and the bad.

Lastly, I'll leave you with this on the subject of hiring. The dental industry loves hiring family or spouses. Actually, 75% of dentists work with a family member during their career. This shocks me! Just because a dentist has a husband or a wife, that does not mean that the husband or wife needs to be the office manager.

Have I seen it work? Yes. But more often than not, it's *rarely* a good business decision. Your employees are put in a difficult position of who to answer to and how to address the right "boss." Home and personal life also get brought to the office when family members work with each other. Listen, we all have our problems, but your other employees and patients should not have to endure them. Trust me, you don't get the "Office Manager of the Century" award for getting married to a dentist.

Again, from the pro-tip I gave you earlier: *Have a role you are hiring for, then hire someone to fit that role. Don't hire someone, then give them a role.* There's someone out there that will be the perfect manager for your dental office, and chances are, they probably aren't your spouse. Food for thought.

I'm not going to get too much in the weeds with this, but with hiring comes the fun department of HR. Consider the new employee paperwork such as contracts, handbooks, HIPAA and OSHA training, and tax paperwork like I-9s, W-4s, and W-2s. Accountants and fractional payroll experts can help here. You don't need your own HR department. Just make sure your business has a process in place for new hires, paperwork, and payroll. This can be created by you, an office manager, or you can consult an HR consultant or fellow colleague.

I hope you enjoyed that journey into my mind. I'm quite passionate about hiring and the effects, positive or negative, your dental team has on your practice. It doesn't matter how skilled you are as a dentist. If you surround yourself with a weak staff, you'll suffer the consequences. Read this chapter over again if that didn't sink in.

Now, let's talk about how to train your dream team.

8

Training

All team members need to be trained in three main areas of your office. Yes, I said your office. Dentists have their own preferences on how they may want to run their practice.

What are these three things to consider when it comes to training?

- Systems and processes
- Roles and responsibilities
- Software

I mentioned that all team members need to be trained on *your* systems and processes because it's your business. You may adopt systems and processes from previous dentists you've worked with, but ultimately, you will have your own playbook. This means you need to ask yourself a few questions.

- How do I want to run my practice day-to-day?
- Do I want my office manager making managerial decisions?
- Do I always want to make managerial decisions alone?
- How is my patient flow going to work from front to back?
- What days am I going to be open and during what hours? Work weekends?
- Who is in charge of ordering supplies?
- Who is responsible for paying bills?
- What are the roles and responsibilities of my front desk administrator(s)?
- What are the roles and responsibilities of my hygienists?
- What are the roles and responsibilities of my assistants?
- What are my monthly and yearly production and collection goals?

Once you have answers to all these questions, write them down! You will learn with experience the best way to run your dental office, but systems and processes can only be finetuned and perfected by writing them down, implementing them, then changing them up as needed. *No* process is perfect the first time you create it.

Systems and Processes Training

Let's review what some basic examples of systems and processes are in any dental office. Remember, a system or process is simply how a certain task is done.

For example, everyone has a process for "How do you make a PBJ?" I'm sure you could write a quick process down for making a PBJ, right?

Keep the "how-to" in mind during this section of the book and imagine writing down, step-by-step, how to do each of these tasks on the admin and clinical side.

How to...

Admin

- Make an appointment
- Confirm appointments
- Perform insurance verification
- Greet, check in, and walk a patient to the back
- Walk out a patient after an appointment
- Create and send claims
- Post all payments
- Research unpaid insurance claims
- Reconcile all payments

Clinical

- Sterilize equipment
- Order supplies
- Take x-rays
- Create treatment plans for patients

- Clean and set up a hygiene operatory for the next patient
- Clean and set up a doctor operatory for the next patient

Remember, these are all examples, and I'm sure you can come up with many other administrative and clinical tasks that are done on a daily basis. Trust me, I know what you're saying. "Really? I seriously have to write down a process for something simple like taking an x-ray?" You don't have to, but it will help *tremendously*.

Having these processes written down significantly decreases any room for error. Any new employee can train under a current employee and follow set processes.

All employees will always have the process to fall back on if anything is forgotten or something falls through the cracks. Systems and processes are proactive measures to running a successful dental office and having a successfully trained dental team.

Roles and Responsibilities

It's imperative to have all roles and responsibilities written out for each position in your dental office. What tasks are that employee responsible for on a daily basis in your practice?

For instance, a hygienist is responsible for "x" daily. An insurance coordinator is responsible for "y" daily. Notice I didn't say any certain name.

So say you have a hygienist named Sandy. These roles and responsibilities aren't Sandy's roles and responsibilities. They are the hygienist's roles and responsibilities because Sandy is a hygienist. Roles and responsibilities should be name-agnostic, as a name doesn't define a role. A role is simply filled by a person with a name.

Everyone remembers his or her first job. How wonderful would it have been if you were handed a list of your daily tasks, when they were supposed to be completed, and how to perform them all? There is no confusion; there is no gray area. Training is still necessary, either by video or in person, but the job roles and responsibilities lay the foundation for clarity.

When a job comes with systems, processes, and training, and there is a physical reference to these day-to-day responsibilities, there is no room for failure.

Software Training

Learning software online is difficult for some team members, so many dentists bring in software trainers to train the team for a few days. I recommend *not* seeing patients on these days! This gives your team time to process the software training without the worry and angst of a patient in front of you at the same time.

I have received kickback on this philosophy over the years. A chief concern for doctors, when either switching software or starting a new practice with a new software, is "taking a day or two to train my team on this software is eating into my production." Well, yeah, but that's a short-sighted way of thinking about it. And yes, you better believe I have solutions to this.

The best way to think of training is with the word "investment." If your team understands how to use your dental software efficiently, it *will* increase overall revenue due to the lessening of errors from poor training. All tasks such as scheduling appointments, creating and updating patient charts, data entry, and insurance verification are done confidently and accurately when your team is trained and knowledgeable. Also, fewer billing mistakes are made, and the overall flow of patients from front to back is seamless. Pay your staff and pay a trainer to make sure your office is confident with their dental software knowledge.

Here's a firsthand example of what I'm talking about:

Back in 2010, I was running an office in South Carolina. We were switching from a web-based software called Dentisoft to a server-based software called OpenDental. Keep in mind this office was part of a small DSO, so it wasn't like my dentist or I were calling the shots.

We were informed, on a Thursday, that we would be switching software that following Monday. What?! Not cool, not cool at all. The only inkling of "thinking ahead" with some basic common sense was a scheduled 30-minute webinar with an OpenDental trainer, showing us the ropes. This webinar was on that same Thursday. *Let me be clear.*

Thirty minutes is not enough time to learn the ins and outs of a new software.

Whether you are on the clinical or administrative side of the dental office, the magic number is four to eight hours of software training. The training should include your team entering in patients, creating fake appointments, entering in treatment plans, walking patients out, creating claims, entering in procedures, and all that good stuff that falls into the typical day-to-day of working in any practice management software.

Although very important, I would venture to say the last thing you really need to learn is how to locate and run various reports. Learn reporting during these training sessions when patients aren't in front of you, the phone isn't ringing off the hook, and you're trying to send claims, collect payments, or present treatment plans.

Wait, I'm fired up and not done yet! Don't try to learn a practice management dental software on the fly when everything I just mentioned is going on.

That's exactly how that first Monday was for my team and me. Patients were more difficult to check in and walk out. The clinical team wasn't familiar enough with entering procedures or using the imaging software, and virtually everything was just out of whack.

This caused us to take longer with every patient, make mistakes, get behind, and ultimately be at the office until 8:00 p.m. that night. We had to reschedule two crown appointments and two hygiene appointments that we simply just couldn't get to, or maybe the patient just decided to leave because of the wait.

Don't make this same mistake. Those four incomplete appointments totaled $2,800 in production. Wouldn't it have been easier to just bring us all in on the previous Friday for four to eight hours, pay (invest in) the staff and familiarize us with the software? Trust me, this would have helped avoid the "run around the office like chickens with our heads cut off" episode that occurred the following Monday.

Also, did you see how we ended up losing $2,800 in production, yet most dentists' biggest fear is using a production day to train on software?

Alright, I've beat a dead horse with this one, but surely you catch my drift.

Solution for Converting Software

1. Pick a weekend day or another day you are typically off to put your team through training.
2. If you have to use a normal work day, clear the schedule, and agree on a day in the future to make up the production. (i.e., open up for one Saturday to reschedule patients)

9

Competitive Analysis

I don't want to get all cutthroat here, as most dentists are not, but if you are reading this book, you clearly care about your success as a dentist. I highly doubt you want to be last on the list of preferred dentists in your area. Who would? So if that's the case, how do you ensure success? What are ways you can set yourself apart, or at least keep up with the competition?

The dental market shouldn't be looked at any differently than other businesses when it comes to competitive analysis. Competitive analysis involves identifying competitors in your area (other dentists) and researching their different marketing strategies. Conducting competitive analysis is not only vital for matching your competitors, but it also helps give you an edge.

Again, we don't live in a world where Dr. Smiley and Dr. Molar are duking it out for patients, bad-mouthing each other like today's politicians with a secret mutual hatred. That is where dental may be different from other businesses. But, we have to discuss the subtle elephant in the room. Both of these doctors would like to do as well or better than the other, especially if they think of the other as competition. This takes me to my next point.

What should you focus on when conducting a competitive analysis? Here are a few basics for you:

1. What is your level of service, and what kind of provider are you?

There is no reason for general dentists to compare themselves to periodontists, endodontists, or other specialties. Different providers provide different services.

Let's say you are a general dentist. You need to find out what most general dentists do in your area and market and how much they charge for various procedures. Is there a reason that a normal customer (patient) would go to one doctor as opposed to another doctor? Could it be that another doctor offers a product like Invisalign, Botox, or dental implants? These are questions you want to ask yourself.

You can always add to your repertoire of skills and provide advanced procedures or products. Don't just do it because other dentists may do it, though. Make the decision that best fits the type of provider you want to be. I've seen multiple dentists spend the money and get the certifications to provide products, such as Invisalign or Botox, only to not understand how to advertise or make time for them in their schedule.

2. What kind of marketing or advertising should you do?

Dentists typically have a hodgepodge of ways to market. I'm sure you've seen the billboards, heard the radio ads, and watched the videos on social media. These are all effective ways of marketing your practice. Don't get behind here. As a business owner, you need to market your dental office. I'm not saying you have to do it all, but find out what works best for you and put your name, or business name, out there. The more people hear about you, the more they remember you. Also, other than social media, put some money into an online presence. Build a professional website—one that answers your potential patients' questions, is informational, easy to navigate, and good-looking. Include patient testimonials and videos if you can. Do your best to speak to what the patient can expect, not what "you" do specifically. What I mean by this is use "you" statements as opposed to "I or we" statements.

For example: "You will enjoy a wonderful experience and a healthy smile." As opposed to "I will give you a wonderful experience and a healthy smile."

Remember, it's not about you; it's about your patients.

One thing I see over and over is dentist websites that literally don't provide any information. Maintaining a working, informational, polished website is a direct reflection of your professionalism and whether or not you cut corners. Please don't be one of those doctors that have "coming soon" on the About Us page for two years. This looks sloppy and indirectly speaks to the type of practice that that dentist operates. Sorry, but it's true.

Insurance Marketing

Another key form of marketing is participating with insurance companies. This is probably the easiest form of marketing for most dentists. Being a preferred participating provider (PPO) means that you are in-network with an insurance company. Being in-network means you have agreed to a contract with an insurance provider and with that contract comes a "set of fees" for various dental procedures that you are obligated to charge a patient with that insurance. This set of fees is called a "fee schedule."

Fee schedules are a listing of fees used by insurance companies to pay doctors at their specific contracted in-network rates. We will cover fee schedules in detail in chapter 12.

These in-network rates are almost always lower than what a dentist or office would charge a cash patient (a patient with no insurance) or a patient with insurance you are *not* in-network with. Long story short: the patient gets a discount for seeing a doctor that's in-network with their insurance.

For example, let's say you are in-network with Metlife, and you have a Metlife patient coming in for a cleaning. Your typical standard fee for a prophy is $100. That's what you would charge a cash patient or an out-of-network patient. However, you are in-network with Metlife, and the Metlife contracted fee for a prophy is $70. In this case, you can only charge the patient $70. Therefore, the patient technically gets a $30 discount by coming to you, the in-network provider.

The example shows why being in-network is basically marketing. The insurance company essentially tells its policyholders who is in-network in the area, and then the policyholder decides who to go to. So although you, the dentist, take a hit on how much you can charge the patient, you still get the patient as a customer.

3. What kind of digital technology will you use in your dental practice?

Again, this falls into what kind of provider you want to be, but technology plays a *big* part in the dental office. Advanced practice management software and imaging software can set your office apart from others. Things like using televisions to show x-rays to patients while sitting in the dental chair lead to far greater case acceptance and more revenue for you.

You can also use advancements in technology as it relates to digital marketing. In chapter five, I discussed products like DemandForce and VYNE Trellis. This form of digital marketing is used for appointment reminders and confirmations. It's used for marketing efforts such as giveaways and free consultations or specials on free products. They make life easier, free up your employees' time to focus attention elsewhere, and make it easy for patients to remember you and their actual dental appointments.

Let me set the stage. Fast forward six months into owning and running your dental practice. And when doing your competitive analysis, you decided *not* to have any of this advanced technology.

And ... action!

Imagine you see Dr. Grill (great dental name, by the way) across the street, adding to her practice. You see the five-star reviews online for Dr. Grill Family Dentistry, and when peeking out your window, you see *everyone* leaving with smiles on their faces and a bunch of dental swag. What goes through your head? You know Dr. Grill invested in some modern technology. Hell, she gave you a tour of the office! The stuff was pretty cool. You can see how it would be nice to have, but it was another expense. Should you have invested in the same stuff?

And ... end scene.

This isn't to scare you; it's just an example to get you to think about technology as an investment, not an expense. However, another investment is simply yourself. *Ultimately, do good dentistry, be fair, and your patients won't leave you*. This builds patient loyalty, and that is the most important relationship to build with patients. Trust builds loyalty. Offer second opinions if a patient is coming from a different office. It's up to you what you charge for your chair time. So if you don't nickel and dime here, and the patient comes to you for the procedure, you win.

But, think about what you need to make life easier for you, your team, and your patients. We live in a fast-paced world. Don't get stuck in the dark ages. If there are easy tools out there to save time and money and increase your bottom line, don't hesitate to use them. Too many dentists I see have the "change isn't good" mentality. This mentality will leave you behind your colleagues.

10

Marketing and Advertising

Like any business, marketing and advertising will play a part in generating revenue in your practice.

For you know-it-alls reading this, let's get something out of the way quickly. I know and understand that marketing and advertising are not the same thing, but they go hand in hand. You are a dentist, so it's pretty self-explanatory what you all do and who your market is. So for this chapter, just do me a solid and think of marketing and advertising as a unit. Here's a quick explanation, though.

In basic terms, marketing is the process of identifying customer (patient) needs and determining how best to meet those needs. In contrast, advertising is the exercise of promoting your dental office and the services you offer through paid channels. In other words, *advertising is a component of marketing*.

You reading this book means you've dreamed of owning your own practice. You've probably even thought of the perfect name for your practice, no different than your first child. Gosh, that's so sweet! You've also thought of a logo, right?

My advice is to have fun with these things, but make them practical. Don't have a super long business name, as it's difficult for people to remember and is not recommended for website URLs.

For your logo, don't lose sleep over this either. You can have something that sets you apart, but names and logos don't make or break dentists. I'm sure you've seen the typical dental offices named "(Fill in the Blank) Family Dental." There is nothing wrong with this. They do just as well as the dentists across the street named "Jagged Tooth Dental" or whatever.

You've also seen the all-too-familiar logo with the various depictions of a tooth. Speaking of this, I need to get something off my chest ... dental office logos remind me of BBQ restaurant logos. *All* BBQ restaurants have some goofy picture of a happy pig on its sign, eating. Why the hell are pigs happy to be eating themselves? Surely I'm not the only one that's noticed this. If you haven't noticed, you can't unsee it once you do.

Pigs and BBQ restaurants … what's wrong with this guy? Anyway, you get the point. Your logo isn't the end all be all of your practice. Many dentists have similar toothy logos, and it has no effect on their practice whatsoever.

You will have a social media and web presence along with plenty of other outlets that require the use of your branding and logo. Just be sure your brand represents your vibe, and your logo is how you want to present your practice to the world, then roll with it.

Creating a name for your business is free. Yay! Your logo will run you anywhere from $150–$400 depending on who you use, and it should be a one-time fee. There are many online companies that will do a perfectly good job of designing a viable logo that will work for you.

Once you have your design, you will receive the vector file of your logo and can send this file to any vendor you use to create advertising and marketing materials.

How should you approach your marketing?

First, set a budget for your marketing and advertising. There's a ton of information on the web about marketing for dentists, so I'm not going to reinvent the wheel here, but there are a few key points I will hit on. Generally speaking, a startup will have to devote a larger percentage of revenue to marketing than an established practice.

This makes sense if you're the new guy. New start-up offices have less revenue per month than an established office. So using $10,000/month to spend, as an example, would mean a $10,000 monthly marketing spend is a greater revenue percentage for a new office than someone already established with more revenue. Follow me?

Before we dive all the way in, here's a refresher of the different avenues through which dentists spend money on marketing and advertising. You can use your marketing budget however you like, and how you use it will greatly depend on where you are, the type of provider you are, and what patients you are trying to attract.

Marketing/Advertising Avenues

- Website
- Insurance marketing (being in-network with insurance companies. Discussed in chapter nine)
- Ad words (Google and social media)
- Radio ads
- Mailers
- TV commercials (rare)
- Billboards
- Magazines
- Word-of-mouth

I left word-of-mouth last so we could talk about it a bit more. It's crucial your office has a good reputation. Why? People talk. People tweet, snap, post, gossip, and love to have their opinions heard. Do your best to make their opinions favorable. Good patients typically talk to and bring other good patients to you. It's science.

Alright, let's discuss marketing budgets. Below, I'm going to split this section up into "what the research says online" and "what I actually see" when it comes to marketing for dentists. Remember, my billing company, Dental ClaimSupport, has worked with thousands of offices across the United States, so we have seen it all.

What the Research Says Online

The average dentist across the United States, who's been operational for six months or more, spends 15%–30% of gross revenue on marketing.[1] Note: I personally think this is very high and should only relate to brand new dentists opening their doors or very highly competitive markets in high standard of living areas. I'll explain in a bit with *real* collected data.

Here are some examples using the different percentages. Large groups and specialty offices tend to have a larger marketing budget as groups compete for as many patients as possible and specialties compete with a smaller number of competitors. If there are more competitors for patients to choose from, your marketing better be good to set yourself apart. Okay, let's look at an example of a monthly marketing budget using 15% of gross revenue as the constant. I used 15% because no one should be spending more than this, even though the research online has shown that some do.

Example of monthly costs in marketing at a 15% level:

1. $500,000 (gross rev) x 15% = $75,000 (or $6,250/month)
2. $1,000,000 (gross rev) x 15% = $150,000 (or $12,500/month)
3. $2,000,000 (gross rev) x 15% = $300,000 (or 25,000/month)

Again, I gathered this info from Dental Economics and Patient Prism,[2] the references you will see at the end of this chapter.

What I Actually See

For this book, I polled 20 different dentists, all clients of my company, Dental ClaimSupport, and in various states across the US. This is what I came up with. From the poll, these dentists have a marketing budget of 2%–4%

of their overall revenue; some are even lower, believe it or not. This should be music to your ears.

Here is the same basic example from earlier, but with the numbers from my poll of 2%–4%:

1. $500,000 (gross rev) x 2% = $10,000 (or $833/month)
2. $1,000,000 (gross rev) x 3% = $30,000 (or $2,500/month)
3. $2,000,000 (gross rev) x 4% = $80,000 (or $6,666/month)

Wow! Those numbers look drastically different and far better for your wallet, don't they? Why is there such a discrepancy? Well, it's not rocket science; many dentists just spend a little too much on marketing, and they don't track dollars spent with what that spend has brought them. I'm not trying to sound flippant or like a wiseass, but that's the truth.

Aside from the averages in our examples, how should your marketing budget really be determined? Thankfully, there is an easy and more precise way to look at this. The answer is return on investment (ROI).

Return on Investment (ROI). Return on investment is a simple performance measure represented as a percentage and is used to evaluate the efficiency or profitability of an investment. Here is the ROI formula:

ROI = (Net Profit/Cost of Investment) x 100

Your mindset needs to be focused on ROI. You can gradually increase what you invest in marketing and measure the return on investment. For example, let's say you invest $2,000 and that investment brings you in $4,000. That would be a 100% ROI. Let's take a look:

$4,000 value - $2,000 investment =
$2,000 profit

($2,000 profit / $2,000 investment) x 100 =
100% ROI

That's a positive ROI, right? So, if you invest $3,000 or $4,000 a month and continue to see a positive ROI, that's fine.

However, once you see a flat or diminishing return, don't invest more in marketing each month.

Dentists measure return on investment in a couple of different ways because dentists really only have to market to get new patients or promote a new product they offer, such as implants. So for this book's sake, let's make it simple.

1. If you are marketing to bring in new patients:

   New patient revenue - Marketing $ spent = $ Return on investment

2. If you are marketing a new product, you offer:

   New product revenue - Marketing $ spent = $ Return on investment

Obviously, if the return on investment is negative, then it was a bad investment. Easy peasy, right?

Golden Rule of Dental Marketing

As long as there is a positive return on investment, it doesn't matter how much you spend. Just make sure your dental practice has the capacity to see the new patients or supply the new product coming in from your marketing efforts.

[1] www.dentaleconomics.com/macro-op-ed/article/16391682/the-new-dentists-guide-to-a-successful-marketing-budget

[2] blog.patientprism.com/dental-marketing-budget

Part 2

And So It Begins … What Happens After the Practice Purchase?

11

Credentialing

Get this process started ASAP!!!! Yes, I put four exclamation points, and I was shouting. This is important, so listen up!

Credentialing is a process that insurance companies use to verify a doctor's legitimacy in education, training, and professional experience. This ensures that the doctor meets the insurance company's internal requirements for serving as an in-network provider on their panel.

That's a mouthful, I know. In layman's terms, "getting credentialed" with an insurance company is like a contract, agreement, or handshake. It also acts as a certain quid pro quo.

Pro-tip: ***If you are going to be an in-network provider with insurance companies,***

this will be your best and easiest marketing effort to increase your patient base.

When credentialed as an in-network provider with the insurance company, a doctor agrees to the terms of the contract, such as certain negotiated fees for procedures (fee schedules covered in the next chapter) and other plan guidelines, such as the authority for the insurance to audit the dental office for compliancy. In turn, the insurance company lists the doctor as an in-network provider on their list of providers. This is insurance marketing because when patients are searching for a provider close to them and in their network, the insurance company will recommend that doctor to the patient.

Too many times, doctors start the credentialing process way too late. You do not have to wait until you've set foot in your new office to start the credentialing process. This is a common misconception of credentialing. In fact, you seriously need to start the process as soon as you have the items outlined in the upcoming credentialing chart. Start this as far in advance of your "first day" in the office as possible.

Before you start the process, you need to do an analysis or pay a credentialing specialist or company to do an analysis. This analysis shows you who the biggest companies are in your area and what insurance they offer. The closer in proximity to your office location, the better. As discussed in chapter nine, credentialing is essentially insurance marketing. You being listed as an in-network provider with insurance drives patients with that insurance to your practice.

To begin the process, you need a few things, though...

Credentialing Info You Will Need

Doctor's Info	Practice Info
• Legal name • Date of birth • Social Security number (SSN) • Degree (DMD vs. DDS) • NPI (Type 1) • Dental license • Resume • Drug Enforcement Agency (DEA) registration number • Proof of liability insurance	• Legal office name and DBA • Signed W-9 • Tax ID • Physical address • Billing address • Phone number • Fax number • Group NPI (Type 2), if applicable

I mean, this sounds reasonable, right? Trust me, I agree. It's absurd all the information you need, but once you have it, well, you have it.

However, on a positive note, this information can also be obtained via the wonderful abbreviation CAQH, also known as the Council for Affordable Quality Healthcare.

The American Dental Association (ADA) teamed up with this wonderful CAQH and created a platform for all US licensed dentists to enter and share their personal and practice data (all that info in the above chart) with dental plans and other healthcare organizations. Therefore, once a doctor's personal and practice info is entered into the CAQH database, it will always be there. It will significantly reduce the administrative burden of gathering this information again for credentialing purposes.

So if you're a dentist and use an outside credentialing service, and you have already entered all your info into CAQH, you've basically done most of the work already without all the back-and-forth. At this point, you'll just need the credentialing specialist to obtain your signatures for a few documents and get the ball rolling.

How long does credentialing take?

Great question. Credentialing can take up to 180 days, but most credentials fall between the 60–120 day range. Why? No one really knows. When your specialist is following up on submitted credentialing paperwork, many credentialing departments just say, "Yes, we received all your information, and it's in process. Sorry, we are backed up."

I swear Justin Timberlake could get credentialed in one day with no hiccups. Seriously. I'm not bitter, though...

Moving on. Providers, prepare for carpal tunnel. Tons of documentation need your John Hancock. That's why using the same credentialing specialists with your same info on file for future credentials can speed up and alleviate this already annoying, sluggish process. Oh, and don't forget about the CAQH we discussed as a means of saving your personal and practice data.

How much does credentialing cost?

Another great question! I'm glad I asked. Credentialing will run you $150/$350 per provider per insurance company. Keep in mind that this includes the credentialing specialist to collect your information, submit all the documentation accurately, and follow up to make sure the application was received and is in process and running smoothly. Many times, this requires multiple phone calls to push the application through, or a fire needs to be lit under the insurance's ass.

Once credentialed, you will receive a notification from the insurance with the effective date and fee schedules associated. You may also be given login credentials for their web portal. Insurance web portals are great tools to utilize for insurance verification, claim research, and claims submission for your dental team.

Re-credentialing and Termination of Contract

Yep, these are real things. Sometimes your credentialing status carries an expiration date. This is when you need to get re-credentialed with that insurance. Indeed this is annoying, but it does make sense because providers' information changes all the time.

Re-credentialing

Re-credentialing is the process insurance companies use to determine that your license is in good standing, that you are qualified according to their eligibility criteria, and that they have all your updated information.

Re-credentialing typically takes place every two to three years, depending on the insurance. Don't sweat it, though, because the insurance company will send you a reminder four to six months before this process would need to be completed. Many offices just throw this mail away or overlook the email, so don't be like them! Have a designated person in your office in charge of mail and on the lookout for important notices.

What you'll need for re-credentialing is:

1. Any changes to your billing or physical address
2. Your up-to-date dental license
3. Your up-to-date DEA license
4. Anything else they may have changed since you were last credentialed (phone number, fax number)

I know what you're wondering, and the answer is no. This does not take as long as getting credentialed in the first place. Yay! This process may only take 30–60 days.

Termination of Contract

Sometimes you need to get out-of-network with an insurance company. This could be because you aren't happy with the contract, or maybe there just aren't enough patients in your area covered by that insurance. Whatever the case, termination of contract is quite simple, but certain important actions need to take place.

You, of course, need to inform the insurance, and you can do this by sending a letter to the provider relations department requesting to terminate the contract. Much like credentialing itself, you need to follow up with the insurance company and confirm they received your termination letter. The insurance will then send you back an effective date of termination, or you will need to call to get this date. It can take roughly two to three months to terminate a contract.

Lastly, and very importantly, you must also inform your patients. You can do this with a letter as well, sent to the patients affected, but also put a notice up in your office of when you expect this to take place. It's unwise not to communicate this to the affected patients because their out-of-pocket expenses and benefit coverage will undoubtedly change once you are out of network with their insurance. If you don't inform these affected patients, they will not be happy campers.

12

Fee Schedules

You've now learned about insurance marketing (chapter nine), how insurance marketing is a leading marketing tool (chapter 10), and how being credentialed builds your patient base by entering into a contract to accept certain fees (chapter 11). There was a reason for the calculated yet flawless lead-in to this chapter covering fee schedules.

Fee schedules are sometimes an afterthought of offices. I can't stand it. They are far more important than offices realize for many reasons, which we'll discuss.

A fee schedule is "a list of the prices of dental procedures." That's it. Now, there's more to fee schedules, but that's all they really are. Here's an example page of an insurance fee schedule:

CDT	Description	General
D0120	Periodic Oral Examination	$31
D0140	Limited Oral Evaluation Problem Focused	$41
D0145	Oral Evaluation – Patient Under 3	$28
D0150	Comprehensive Oral Examination	$43
D0160	Detailed and Extensive Oral Evaluation (Problem Focused)	$55
D0180	Comprehensive Periodontal Evaluation	$52
D0210	Intraoral – Complete Series (Including Bitewings)	$100
D0220	Intraoral – Periapical – First Radiographic Image	$21
D0230	Intraoral – Periapical – Each Additional Radiographic Image	$18
D0240	Intraoral – Occlusal Radiographic Image	$26
D0250	Extra–oral – 2D Projection Radiographic Image Created Using a Stationary Radiation Source, and Detector	$45
D0270	Bitewing – Single Radiographic Image	$20
D0272	Bitewings – Two Radiographic Images	$30
D0273	Bitewings – Three Radiographic Images	$32
D0274	Bitewings – Four Radiographic Images	$39
D0277	Vertical Bitewings – 7 to 8 Radiographic Images	$66
D0330	Panoramic Radiographic Image	$76
D0340	2D Cephalometric Radiographic Image – Acquisition, Measurement and Analysis	$74
D0460	Pulp Vitality Tests	$30
D0470	Diagnostic Casts	$41
D1110	Prophylaxis – Adult	$55
D1120	Prophylaxis – Child	$38
D1206	Topical Fluoride Varnish for High Caries Risk Patients	$25
D1208	Topical Fluoride – excluding Varnish	$24
D1351	Sealant – per Tooth	$32
D1352	Preventive Resin Restoration	$33
D1353	Sealant Repair - Per Tooth	$30
D1354	Interim Caries Arresting Medicament Application - Per Tooth	$25
D1510	Space Maintainer – Fixed Unilateral	$190
D1516	Space Maintainer – Fixed – Bilateral, Maxillary	$280
D1517	Space Maintainer – Fixed – Bilateral, Mandibular	$280
D1550	Re–cementation or Re–bond of Space Maintainer	$45
D1555	Removal of Fixed Space Maintainer	$39
D1575	Distal Shoe Space Maintainer – Fixed – Unilateral	$190
D2140	Amalgam – One Surface, Primary or Permanent	$80
D2150	Amalgam – Two Surfaces, Primary or Permanent	$92
D2160	Amalgam – Three Surfaces, Primary or Permanent	$112
D2161	Amalgam – Four Surfaces, Primary or Permanent	$132

As you can see, there is the CDT (Current Dental Terminology) code on the far left, the description of the code in the middle, and the fee amount on the far right. There really isn't anything else to it.

So that's an insurance fee schedule, but every office also has its own standard fee schedule, sometimes called the office fee schedule. These mean the same thing. This is what the office would charge a cash patient with no insurance or a patient with insurance with which the office doesn't participate or, in other words, is out-of-network.

Also, every insurance you do participate with would have its own fee schedule too. Remember when I talked about how being in-network means a doctor agrees to the terms of the contract, such as *certain negotiated fees for procedures*? That's exactly why you have a separate fee schedule for every insurance you are in-network with.

Let's make this even simpler: say you are in-network with only two insurances, Metlife and Guardian. Because you have a standard fee schedule, too, you will have three fee schedules associated with your office.

1. Standard fee schedule (office fee schedule)
2. Metlife fee schedule
3. Guardian fee schedule

Every fee schedule you have needs to be entered into your practice management software (PMS) and applied accurately to respective patients. From our previous example, this means:

- Patients with Metlife insurance will have the Metlife fee schedule applied to their patient account.
- Patients with Guardian insurance will have the Guardian fee schedule applied to their account.
- All other patients will have the standard fee schedule applied to their accounts.

Goodness, I know this sounds redundant, but tons of offices mess this up, and it leads to incorrect billing, inaccurate calculations, and disgruntled patients.

Do you ever need to update these fee schedules?

Yep! Fee schedules should be updated in your PMS whenever the insurance updates and sends a new fee schedule. The insurance would inform you of this by email or mail. Insurances will go up or increase their price on certain fees every now and then to keep up with inflation and provide fair reimbursement. This can be every one to two years, depending on the insurance. If you don't update these fees, your overall numbers will be incorrect. I will explain in a second.

Important note: *When accurately entered and used correctly, fee schedules tell us exactly what the patient's highest allowable charges are.*

For instance, in the office example where we are in-network with Metlife and Guardian only, a Metlife patient's highest allowable charge can only be what the Metlife fee schedule says it is for any particular procedure. If your standard office fee for a prophy is $100 and the Metlife fee for that same procedure is $70, a Metlife patient can only be charged $70—meaning they get a discount of $30 for going to an in-network provider.

Insurance would most likely pay this procedure at $70, *but* if the procedure was not covered for whatever reason, that patient would only come out of pocket $70, not the $100 office fee. The office would have to "write off" or "adjust" $30 if the patient were charged $100.

$100 (office fee) - $70 (in-network fee) = ***$30 (write-off)***

Accurate fee schedules also help with:

- Accurate production numbers
- Forecasted collections
- Proper treatment presentation (showing discounts and accurate savings but also correct patient out-of-pocket expenses)
- Correct adjustments (insurance write-offs) for single or dual insurance patients

Don't take these bullet points lightly! Many doctors across the US struggle terribly with understanding their true numbers. An easy example is production numbers. If an office produces $1,000,000 in production but has to write off $100,000 in insurance adjustments (like in the example before), what is the "true" production? True production is commonly referred to as "net production."

$1 mil (production) - $100k (insurance adjustments) = ***$900,000 (net production)***

Far too often, I hear doctors, in a case like this, say their production and what they expect to collect is $1 million. Sorry, but that's impossible.

You can *only* collect up to your "net production," so in this case, you are only entitled to $900,000. You see how that doctor could be sorely disappointed year in and year out? This is a common error doctors make when referring to their production.

And lastly, fee schedules contribute to overall ease in treatment planning, case presentation, case acceptance, and accurate accounting.

Yes, if fee schedules are accurate, your dental team can show patients what they are "saving," and patients are far more inclined to schedule the treatment. This means more money for you!

Your billing team can confidently and swiftly post insurance payments with correct write-offs because the fees are correct. Patient accounts are clean. What does that mean? It means patients are far less likely to get upset and dispute dental bills.

I say all this because inaccurate fee schedules lead to incorrect patient ledgers. Bad accounting or billing is the leading cause of losing patients and revenue. Don't be that kind of office.

13

Practice Management Software

What practice management software should you choose? This is a big decision that, in my opinion, some dentists don't take seriously enough. From my experience, dentists feel it's all the same. Guess what? Not all practice management software is the same! Also, for the sake of writing "PMS" or "practice management software" again and again, I'm just going to refer to it as "dental software."

Why would I devote a chapter to dental software in a book about starting a practice? Because I think it's extremely important, that's why! Having a skilled team and proper training is already difficult enough. Don't add to the complexity by using inferior software. I have seen offices struggle because of a certain dental software. Bad reporting, extra load times, compatibility with imaging software, and poor customer support are all items that can hinder your dental team when working in any dental software.

The top three most-used dental software programs out there right now are Dentrix, Eaglesoft, and Opendental. My personal favorite is OpenDental, and there's not even a close second. Again, not all dental software is the same, but they should perform the same functions. Some are just more intuitive and user-friendly.

How do most dentists choose their dental software?

Many dentists elect to go with Dentrix if they get their supplies from Henry Schein; likewise with Eaglesoft if you get supplies from Patterson. This is because these supply companies own their own dental software. But you don't have to do this.

Do some research yourself by poking around websites and watching training videos on each software. You wouldn't just resign yourself to using Safari if you had a

MacBook, would you? No, you might still use Google Chrome as your browser because you like it more.

We actually polled our whole team at Dental ClaimSupport, asking them their favorite dental software. Remember, DCS is an outsourced dental billing company, so our team isn't just blowing smoke. People get very biased as it relates to dental software, so the numbers I'm going to provide below are feisty, passionate votes for favorite software. Seriously, it's a little ridiculous when people get on soap boxes about their favorites or not-so favorites. There can be real hatred toward some. Ha!

Here you go:

1st Place	OpenDental
2nd Place	Dentrix
3rd Place	Eaglesoft
4th Place	Curve

For the record, I 100% agree with first place: OpenDental. The speed and navigation of the software are unmatched. They also paid particular attention to the billing functions of the software. I say this because many programs are clinical-driven, meaning it favors the doctors and hygienists, but can be a pain in the butt for your administration team up front. OpenDental does the best job of being an all-around effective software in form and function for small, medium, or large practices or groups with multiple locations.

So you know I'm not just making things up, take a look at this article when you have some time: *www.dentalclaimsupport.com/blog/best-dental-practice-management-software*

Please remember what you read in chapter eight about training. Your team needs to understand the ins and outs of your PMS. Their level of expertise will directly affect your revenue, trust me. Set aside time for software training if you are opening your doors or switching software in the future.

14

Your Appointment Book

You know what a gorgeous sight is? A full appointment book with new and established patients!

It literally screams success. It means marketing efforts have worked. It means patients are talking to other patients about you (remember word of mouth?)

It means money. Yeah, I said it.

Don't get all giddy yet. You and your team need to know how to schedule patients properly and how to handle a full schedule. A full appointment book doesn't do anything for you if you aren't set up operationally.

For success, have your dental team complete the following tasks for every scheduled patient.

1. Confirm that the patient is coming in for their scheduled appointment.
2. Confirm insurance verification is complete *before* the appointment.
3. Confirm there's coverage for the procedures being performed.
4. Confirm your data entry is correct.

Full schedule or not, the upcoming appointments need to be confirmed to ensure your patients are actually coming into the office. Yes, patients conveniently forget they have dental appointments. So annoying. This hurts your revenue if you neglect to confirm appointments. It's easy too, so there's no excuse. Just pick up the phone or use a text marketing product like Demand Force, mentioned earlier in this book. Also, when confirming appointments and if patients drop off the schedule, you should now have time to fill those voids with other patients needing to get in.

Insurance verification *has* to be performed on all patients. Get a full breakdown of benefits, and ensure the patient is active with coverage before they are seen.

Scheduling patients doesn't seem like a major deal, but it is. There is a science to it, or there should be. Different procedures take different amounts of time to perform. Some providers like to perform higher production (crowns, bridges, implants) in the morning and lower production (fillings, extractions) in the afternoon. Less can go wrong, or should I say, there are fewer surprises with less extensive procedures like fillings and extractions. For those reasons, many dentists prefer these types of procedures in the afternoon to close out their day.

Find out how you prefer your patients scheduled, create a strategy for scheduling your patients the right way, and implement this strategy with your dental team. They and you will know what type and when procedures are being performed and will get comfortable with the time allotment for each procedure.

15

Operations and Dental Billing

Every dental office needs a script for how it operates. We have already been over the roles and responsibilities of dental office team members in chapter eight and also hit on certain functions of the office, such as scheduling patients, in the last chapter. Your operations can be defined as what happens during daily normal office hours.

Does your day start with a morning huddle? How is the first patient taken back to the doctor or hygiene chair? When does the administration team perform insurance verification for patients, and when are your patient and insurance payments posted? How do you close every day out?

These are all questions about various tasks that drive the daily operations of your office.

I've provided a cheat sheet outline of administrative operations and clinical operations. I'm giving you this information because you're reading my book, which hopefully you paid for, and that makes me like you. Kidding!

In all seriousness, you're reading this book because you want to see your practice thrive. This cheat sheet of operational tasks for the admin and clinical teams will outline and help structure your day-to-day operations.

Remember, not every office is run the same, but these are the basic tasks that should be performed in all offices. I have already discussed in chapter eight that all roles and responsibilities should be accompanied by a process for all tasks performed. So when you are going through these operations below, get those creative juices flowing through your brain. Each operation is essentially a task, so think about the process and start to formulate it, then figure out who is accountable for that task.

Start imagining how you will want your office set up. Focus on having the right people in the right roles so you can focus on patients and good dentistry.

When I explain the operations below, I'm not talking about turning on the lights in your practice in the morning, turning on computers, or making coffee. Let's be honest, most people don't want to read books any longer than they should be, so I'll spare you guys. Moving on...

Administrative Operations

1. Morning huddle
    a. Discuss the previous day (Was it good or bad? Any special shout-outs for an employee that went above and beyond? Anything funny to start the day?). Good vibes and positive attitudes are crucial before everyone has had coffee.
    b. Discuss goals for the current day.
    c. Print schedules for the day. Look for:

i. Any unscheduled treatment (patients that need work done but haven't scheduled it yet)?

ii. Any opportunity for same-day treatment (that's moving a hygiene patient to the doctor's chair for work on the same day)? Why have them make another appointment?

iii. Any open appointments that can be filled?

d. What needs to be done for each patient?

i. The hygienist and assistant are responsible for their own schedules.

e. Lab cases: have they been sent off or received?

f. Insurance verification: is it complete for all patients?

g. Any VIPs (very important patients)? These can be patients you love or loathe … Haha! Not kidding—annoying/challenging patients. Seriously, it's good to know who's coming in that day so you can mentally prepare.

h. Briefly discuss the following day (Anything stand out that needs to be mentioned? Big case? Lunch and learn?).

2. Check in the first patient.
3. Send all dental claims from the previous day.
4. While patients are being seen or in allotted time slots, the admin team needs to do these tasks:
   a. Insurance verification (48 hours out)
   b. Payment posting
   c. Claims research
   d. Scheduling patients
   e. Confirming appointments
   f. All data entry (insurance and patient information)
5. Check patients out that have completed appointments and batch dental claims ("batch" means to create dental

claims and put them in a queue to send).

6. Schedule the next appointment.
7. Pay attention to the daily schedule. Try not to get behind!
8. Now, close out your day! You've made it through the schedule, and all patients have been seen.
9. Reconciliation: validate all your payments match (insurance payments, credit cards, patients' checks, cash, etc.), meaning whatever was posted in your dental software matches what's deposited or will be deposited into your bank account.
10. Have your clinical team go over their day sheets.
    a. Assistants go through the doctor's schedule and confirm that procedures done for each patient are accurate and can be billed to patients and insurance companies.
    b. Hygienists go through their own schedules and confirm that proce-

dures done for each patient are accurate and can be billed to patients and insurance companies.

11. Make sure all claims have been created and batched from the day.
12. Quickly go over the schedule for the following day and check for any incomplete tasks (any incomplete insurance verifications or appointment confirmations?).

Clinical Operations

1. Participate in morning huddle (explained in detail in admin operations).
2. Take the first patient back to the hygienist or doctor chair.
    a. Perform necessary procedures.
    b. Take necessary x-rays.
    c. Save x-rays to imaging or PMS software.
3. Complete the appointment and walk the patient out (patient check-out).
    a. This is when some hygienists and assistants elect to enter clinical

notes for the patients rather than wait until later.

4. Clean, sanitize, and prepare hygienist or doctor operatory for the next patient.
5. Clean and sanitize instruments.
6. Confirm patients during downtime. Sometimes the admin team does this. Offices vary.
7. Complete all clinical notes for all patients by the end of the day, if you haven't already (This has to be done!).
8. Assistants and hygienists go over their own day sheets and make sure what was done in the dental chair is reflected on the patient's ledger (same as admin operations item 10).
    a. This ensures procedures attached to claim forms are accurate and billable.
9. Quickly go over the schedule for the following day and check to prepare for your patients.

Well, there you have it. You literally just went through what exact daily operations are in the dental office, well, on paper at least. Having a solid operational foundation will soften the blow of unexpected surprises or emergencies that inevitably arise in the dental office from time to time. Your team will be equipped to handle these challenges.

Dental Billing

I'm a dental nerd, and this is my favorite part of running any dental office. You can produce all the crowns in the world, but if you don't know how to collect from insurance companies or patients, it's all for nothing.

In my previous book, *Ultimate Guide to Dental Billing and Reporting,* which you should read if you haven't already, I explain the full dental billing process from start to finish. I also outline the integral business reports you must understand in order to know if your office is running poorly or, fingers crossed, is running clean and profitable.

The billing process can be summed up in two phases: the "life cycle of a patient" and the "life cycle of a dental claim." For the sake of not having to write the *Ultimate Guide to*

Dental Billing and Reporting book all over again, I'm just going to list the two phases for you.

Here's a link to follow for a copy of the book. 😉 *www.dentalclaimsupport.com/dental-billingandreporting*

Phase 1: Life-Cycle of a Dental Patient

1. The patient makes an appointment and gives insurance and protected health information (PHI) info to your office.
2. Your office enters the patient's PHI into the dental software.
3. Your dental team performs insurance verification before the patient is seen.
4. The patient is seen for the appointment and walked out after the visit.

Phase 2: Life-Cycle of a Dental Claim

1. Your dental team creates the insurance claim, and the claim is batched.

2. The dental claim is sent using a clearinghouse from the dental software to the insurance company.
3. The insurance company processes the claim and makes a payment to your office via an electronic funds transfer (EFT), virtual credit card (VCC), or paper check.
4. Payment is posted in the patient ledger, which closes out the claim.

If you have the right dental team in place with proper training and follow this process, getting paid isn't difficult. Actually, none of this stuff is difficult; it just needs to be done. More often than not, some employees just get lazy and complacent.

I don't enjoy saying that sometimes people just punch a clock to get paid, but that's the reality. Some people just don't give a crap about your office—they just care about their paycheck. Try your best to incentivize your team and make them a part of something special. Have goals. If the goals are hit, spread the wealth. It's not that difficult, and you retain incredible employees.

Amazing employees still need some help sometimes. Remember, our company, Dental ClaimSupport, can eliminate the stress of cumbersome and dreaded insurance billing. This book has encompassed the myriad of activities that drive a dental office. If your office is better suited to outsourcing the insurance billing so you can focus attention on your patients and dentistry, I wouldn't hesitate to outsource.

Sorry, I had to plug my company at the end of the book. It just made sense…

16

Are You Ready?

Well ... you made it! I'm hoping you real-ized this book took a different angle than your traditional dental publications. I personally don't think you need a 200-page book focused only on how to get a loan or how to market your dental practice. Many books explain how to do one thing or another, but they aren't written in layman's terms and easy to understand or relate to.

You may have guessed this book was going to be a lot of what you already knew or just a random thing you could reference now and then. But it's much more than that.

It was designed with *you* in mind and what truly lies ahead for your journey in dentistry. Just because you started a practice from scratch or acquired one in a business purchase doesn't mean you laugh your happy ass all the way to the bank. Nope, quite the contrary. What happens after the ink dries on the contract, and you walk through those doors and stick your hands in patients' mouths is when the real work begins.

You are a phenomenal dentist, no doubt. But are you a phenomenal business owner yet? This book laid out some basics for you to use to begin your entrepreneurial success as a business-owning dentist. Few people receive this type of education in the dental field, so pat yourself on the back and celebrate that you already know what others do not.

It's a known fact that dental students leave school with enormous debt. It's the new norm. Shoot, only as far back as 2010, the average dental student would finish school with anywhere from $100k–$200k in loans to be paid back on a 10-year schedule.

Fast forward to the present…

Dental students are looking at debt anywhere from $300k–$500k and paying it back on a 20–30 year schedule—literally no different than a home mortgage! You just read that, and it probably gave you that uneasy pit in your stomach like you forgot to study for an exam or lost your passport while vacationing in the Sahara. I get it. You are not alone, though.

I can't pay your debts for you, but the concepts and basics you've learned in this book will provide you with a smooth game plan to follow. Don't expect to do everything perfectly when opening up your own practice. You *will* make mistakes; we all do. But following only a small percentage of the advice in this book will significantly decrease the chance of financial blunders—such as not knowing how to collect from insurance companies or severely underestimating expenses—you will encounter as a business owner.

Again, don't make the mistake of expecting your office to be perfect. Implement what you've learned here, revisit as you go, and improve on your processes and strategies.

Remember, I'm not a dentist, but I am a business owner.

Fact: All businesses are the same when you boil it down to infrastructure. It's the same as all people look alike if you only saw their skeletons. The moment you think your business is different is the moment you shoot yourself in the foot.

Dental ClaimSupport made that mistake here early on. I'll never forget our business coach, Greg Gray (awesome guy, by the way) telling my partners and me exactly what I just told you. All businesses are the same. Every business has departments: operations, HR, marketing, IT, sales, etc. Dental offices are no different.

Sure, what exactly happens when printing a T-shirt in a factory is different from performing a crown on a patient. But what's not different is there is a process and a means of moving said T-shirt or patient through that process.

This book is full of real data, expert opinions, and "from the horse's mouth" type of knowledge. You now have a weapon in your arsenal to reference when making financial decisions that affect your new, existing, or future practice.

What else is this book? It's an exercise to get you to think like a business owner and not only as a dentist. Believe me, you do that enough already.

Acknowledgments

Christopher Comer, DMD
Jimmy McIntire, Pan-Am
Tim Blanco, Chatham Insurance
Travis Thomas, South State Bank

www.ingramcontent.com/pod-product-compliance
Lightning Source LLC
LaVergne TN
LVHW020234210926
848481LV00016B/1958
* 9 7 8 1 9 5 4 9 4 3 4 9 0 *